THE NBA

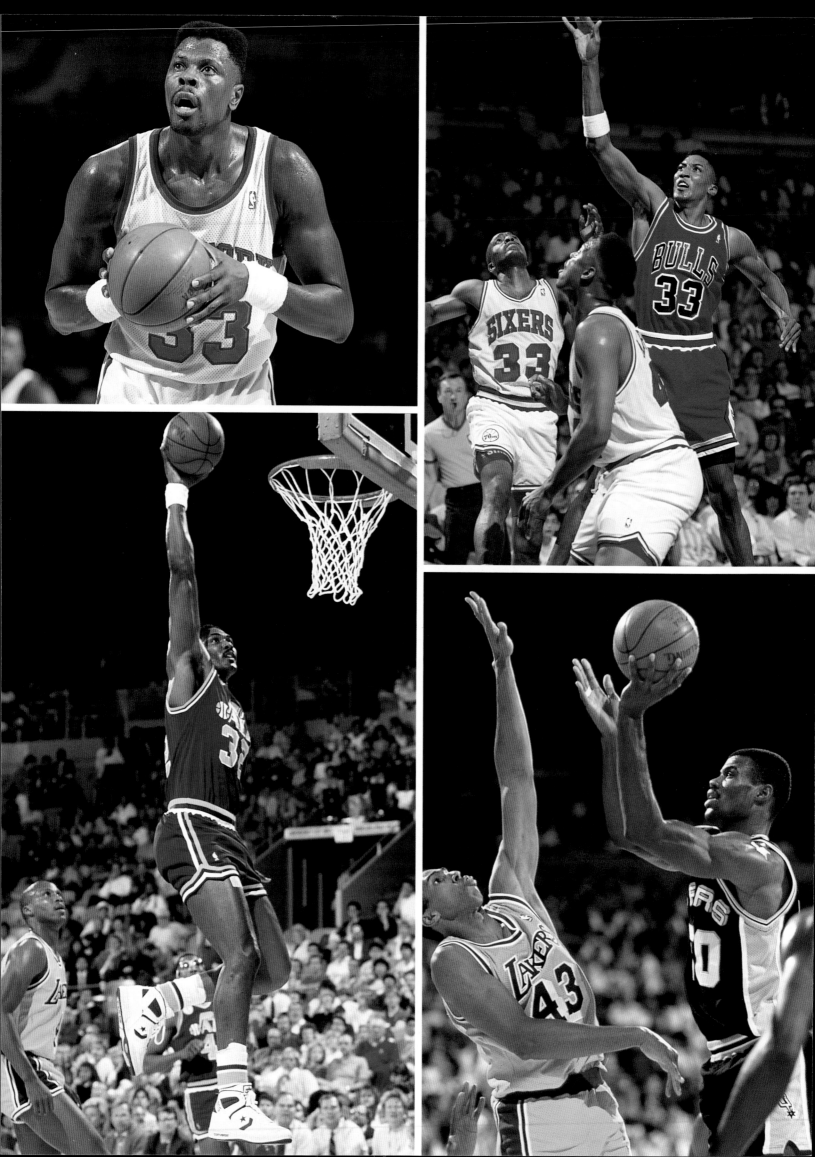

THE NBA

TODAY'S STARS
TOMORROW'S LEGENDS

JACK CLARY

This edition published in 1992 by NDM Publications, Inc.
Great Pond Publishing, Ltd. is an imprint of
NDM Publications, Inc.
30 Inwood Road
Rocky Hill, CT 06067

Produced by Brompton Books Corp.
15 Sherwood Place
Greenwich, CT 06830

ISBN 1-56657-015-8

Printed in Hong Kong

*Michael Jordan (**Page 1**) is
one of the greatest players
in NBA history and he
joined four other great
NBA stars (**Page 2,
clockwise**), Patrick Ewing,
Scottie Pippen, David
Robinson and Karl
Malone, as members of the
1992 U.S. Olympic team. It
was the first time that
America was able to send
its great pro stars to
compete in the Olympics.*

Below: *The 1992 NBA East
All-Star team starters, from
left: Michael Jordan,
Chicago; Isiah Thomas,
Detroit; Scottie Pippen,
Chicago; Patrick Ewing,
New York; Charles
Barkley, Philadelphia;
Kevin Willis, Atlanta.*

Picture Credits

Allsport Photography, Inc: Allsport: 107(bottom); Scott
  Cunningham: 97(top); Jonathan Daniel: 1, 52(bottom), 100;
  Tim DeFrisco: 10, 17, 18(bottom), 19, 33, 35(right),
  37(bottom), 42(bottom), 47(both), 48(bottom right), 57, 63,
  69(bottom), 70, 72(top), 73, 78, 80, 84, 86(top), 94,
  95(bottom), 96, 104(both), 107(top), 108; Stephen Dunn:
  2(bottom left), 11, 58(bottom), 59, 60(left), 62, 111; Otto
  Greule, Jr: 37(top), 69(top); Jim Gund: 20, 48(bottom left),
  49, 83; Ken Levine: 6(right), 7, 24, 30(both), 35(left),
  40(both), 43(bottom), 46, 58, 64, 66, 76, 77(left), 101(right),
  102; Mark Morrison: 77(right); Joe Patronite: 99(top); Mike
  Powell: 2(bottom right), 22, 23(bottom left), 25(top), 26,
  28(top left), 38, 39(both), 65(both), 85(top), 86(bottom); Earl
  Richardson: 8(right); Jim Spoonts: 90; Brian Spurlock: 8(left),
  9(both); Rick Stewart: 105; Damian Strohmeyer: 13(left), 15,
  41, 56, 91, 109; Stephen Wade: 12, 110(bottom).
Bruce Bennett Studios: M. Campanelli: 2(top left); J.
  Giamundo: 29(both); S. Levy: 31, 33, 103(bottom), 106;
  B. Miller: 2(top right), 16.
NBA Hoops: 23(top right), 42(top right), 43(top left), 55(top
  right), 67(top left), 79(top right), 110(top left).
Carl Sissac: 4, 6(left), 14, 18(top), 21, 25(bottom), 27(bottom),
  32(top), 34, 36, 44(both), 45, 48(top), 50(top), 51, 52(top), 53,
  54(top), 55(bottom), 60(right), 61, 65(bottom), 67(bottom),
  68, 71(top), 72(bottom), 74(bottom), 75, 79(bottom), 81, 82,
  87, 88, 89(top), 92, 93(bottom), 95(top), 97(bottom),
  98(both), 99(bottom), 101(left), 103(top).
Skybox Corporation: 13(bottom right), 27(top), 50(bottom
  right), 74(top left), 89(bottom left), 93(top).
Upper Deck: 28(bottom), 71(bottom right), 85(bottom right).

Acknowledgments

It took an all-star team effort to produce this book, beginning
with the cooperation of the public relations directors of the
NBA's 27 teams and its league office. Consultation also was
helpful from Mark Vocca, of NDM Publications, who planted
the seed for this book and whose knowledge of the NBA even
exceeds his love for the Cleveland Cavaliers. Thanks must also
go to managing editor Jean Martin; the editor of this project,
Barbara Thrasher; Kathy Schneider, who researched and
provided an amazing array of color photographs; designer Don
Longabucco; and Jennifer L. Cross, who prepared the index.

CONTENTS

INTRODUCTION

In some ways professional basketball is like Old Man River – it just keeps rollin' along, from year to year, from generation to generation. Exceptional players define the scope of the hoop sport, establishing new records of excellence that stand only until they are broken by the next rising star. But unlike Old Man River, pro basketball is on an upward spiral of popularity and excitement – propelled by ever more talented players and by the media.

This volume focusses on those NBA stars who are at the beginning or pinnacle of their careers – the players who will take the sport to new heights into the new millenium, and who are destined to become basketball's legends of tomorrow. The pantheon of stars includes such well-known players as Michael Jordan, David Robinson, Karl Malone, Reggie Lewis, Tim Hardaway, Shawn Kemp, Brad Daugherty, Chris Mullin, Kevin Johnson, Patrick Ewing, Scottie Pippen, John Stockton, and K.J. Johnson.

In the constant changing of the guard that characterizes any sport, today's stars take their places beside such older and well-respected talents as the Boston Celtics' Big Three of Larry Bird, Kevin McHale and Robert Parish, plus Moses Malone, Tom Chambers, Rolando Blackman, Mo Cheeks and Bernard King, who are in the twilight of their careers. And these players, in turn, had replaced such stars of the seventies and eighties as Julius Erving, Kareem Abdul-Jabbar, George Gervin, Alex English, Bob Lanier, Elvin Hayes, Pete Maravich and Dennis Johnson. It has been this way since the formation of the National Basketball Association in the late forties, when professional basketball finally caught hold on the American sporting public that was eagerly looking for new entertainment and new stars.

Today's masterful athletes of the court, with their grace, coordination and strength, often are compared to such great ballet masters as Mikhail Baryshnikov. Excessive hyperbole? Perhaps ... unless one has watched Michael Jordan and his endless array of airborne antics in which he seems to go several directions at once while on an extemporaneous flight path to the basket ... or has marveled at the elegant movements of 7′ 1″ David Robinson underneath the basket, when he either slams home a dunk shot or leaps, like a striking snake, to block a shot. Those leaps and dunks are born of both talent and hard work, and are as inspiring for those on the court as for those in the stands. These men are a joy to watch.

For the first time ever, the best of America's basketball stars – the men who are masters of this particular ballet – performed in the Olympic Games, showcasing their talents in 1992 for all the world. That group included Michael Jordan and Patrick Ewing, both 1984 gold medal Olympians; David Robinson, a bronze medalist in the 1988 Games; Jordan's teammate, Scot-

tie Pippen; John Stockton and Karl Malone of the Utah Jazz; Charles Barkley, who didn't survive his first Olympic tryout in 1984; Clyde Drexler; Chris Mullin; and two greybeards to whom we here pay tribute – Larry Bird and Magic Johnson.

Those two NBA veterans, who shared the highest level of stardom, made the Olympic Games the curtain call of their illustrious careers. They had brought to the NBA a fierce personal rivalry born in the 1979 NCAA championship game when Johnson's Michigan State Spartans defeated Bird and Indiana State. The rivalry became supercharged over an entire decade because they were the centerpieces of the Boston Celtics and the Los Angeles Lakers, the NBA's two best teams during that time.

That Bird and Johnson were different in so many ways only served to accentuate the rivalry. Bird was blessed with instincts that were among the most marvelous ever seen on a basketball court. Unlike Johnson, his body was not cast in Olympian splendor, but he always had what basketball people call "enough" – enough mobility to score more than 21,000 points as one of the game's most feared shooters while playing the so-called "small forward" position; enough jumping ability to pull down over 9,000 rebounds; enough

court vision to direct passes for almost 6,000 assists. When a game was on the line in the final seconds, he wanted the ball to make the decisive shot – and more often than not, he made it!

Magic – and what more appropriate nickname – had the Olympian body. While leading his Los Angeles Lakers teams to five NBA championships he matched many of Bird's basketball skills and then added two others – great athleticism and the ability to direct his team as a point guard. Before Johnson, players who were 6' 9" never played in the backcourt. But he dispelled that notion with his great ballhandling, laser-like passing and swoops to the basket. While Bird used his all-business, seemingly arrogant, on-court approach to help fuel his competitiveness, Magic rounded off his competitive nature with laughter and fun. His attitude added a pleasant dimension to a game played by multimillionaires who sometimes show too much stone-faced self-importance both on and off the court.

While Johnson proved that 6' 9" players can play guard, that still has not dispelled the role of the so-called "little guys," which in today's NBA parlance means players who are between 6' 1" and 6' 3". Some of those so-called "little guys" also will be stars of the nineties – John Stockton, Mark Price, Dee Brown,

Ron Harper and Michael Adams.

Although most of the stars featured in this volume are at the beginning or peak of their careers, others profiled herein achieved stardom in the mid and late eighties, but promise to work their magic on the court for several years to come. Charter members of the Stars of the Nineties include Olympians such as Charles Barkley and Clyde Drexler; the keystones to Detroit's back-to-back NBA titles, Isiah Thomas and Joe Dumars; James Worthy, who was a member of four Lakers NBA titlists; Hakeem Olajuwon of the Houston Rockets; and Dominique Wilkins of Atlanta.

On the other end of the spectrum, there are the recently emerging stars such as Larry Johnson, the number one pick of the NBA in 1991, who then won Rookie of the Year honors with the Charlotte Hornets; Dikembe Mutombo, also Class of '91, who became a feared center in his rookie season at Denver; and Ron Seikaly, another young center with the Miami Heat.

And, of course, there are the incoming stars. Though too new to the professional circuit to profile in this volume, these young stars display too much talent and promise to dismiss. Add to the list of NBA Stars of the Nineties such players as Shaquille O'Neal from Louisiana State University; Jimmy Jackson from Ohio State; Alonzo Mourning from Georgetown; Harold Miner of Southern California; Christian Laettner and Grant Hill, who helped lead Duke to back-to-back NCAA championships in the early nineties; Malik Sealy from St. John's University in New York City; Don MacLean from UCLA, who has surpassed the accomplishments of two other great Bruins centers, Kareem Abdul-Jabbar and Bill Walton; and Walt Williams from Maryland.

Many believe that Shaquille O'Neal can become one of the greatest players ever. His 7' 1", 300-pound body still must be further toughened for the rigors of an NBA career, and his offensive skills need much more polish. Even before O'Neal got to the NBA, scouts developed a composite of his ability: "He can run the court, he can block shots and he's an awesome physical specimen. He likes to play and he is strong. His offensive refinements will come with experience, and if he improves his foul shooting, he will become a dominant player."

Many are already comparing him to Wilt Chamberlain – one of the greatest centers in basketball history – and some believe he can succeed Jordan as King of the NBA when Michael finally retires.

Former St. John's University coach Lou Carnesecca commented that O'Neal is much like Houston's Hakeem Olajuwon, except that he's bigger. "He's a franchise, no doubt about it," Carnesecca said. "He'd make a good foundation, like the pyramids or St. Peter's Basilica."

Christian Laettner was another great college player. Though not considered as dominating as O'Neal, he was the only collegian selected for the U.S. Olympic team in 1992. At 6′ 11″, 225 pounds, he can play power forward in the NBA with excellence, and he possesses a toughness that always surprises. His skills also caught Carnesecca's attention. "He's very cool and poised," the former St. John's coach said. "He gets better every year and his potential is unlimited to become a fine NBA player."

Laettner's coolness under fire was best exemplified by his dramatic last-second turnaround jump shot against the University of Kentucky in the NCAA championship semifinal in 1992 that propelled Duke to the finals; and in his dramatic second-half performance in the finals against Michigan that enabled the Blue Devils to win their second straight collegiate title.

Alonzo Mourning followed in the footsteps of Patrick Ewing and Dikembe Mutombo at Georgetown, and everyone agrees that he can be a dominating inside player. He was a member of the 1988 U.S. Olympic team, coached by his Georgetown mentor, John Thompson, even before he had played a game for the Hoyas. Mourning has been compared to a mix of Bill Russell and Moses Malone. As a 6′ 10″ forward, he averaged 23 points, 12 rebounds and five blocked shots in his senior year at Georgetown.

"He'll be a great pro," said Seton Hall coach P.J. Carlissimo, who had coached him in international competition, to which Thompson added: "His game is far more suited at the outset to the NBA. He has creative ability on the court that marks the difference between great, big players and ordinary big players. He is a great one-on-one player and that is the name of the game in the pros which do not feature the massed zone defenses he faced in college."

Jimmy Jackson gave up his last year of eligibility to join the NBA in the 1992 draft. But his ability to direct an offense with his great ballhandling and passing skills, and a deadly outside jump shot, set him apart from every other collegiate guard.

Walt Williams is cut in the physical mold of Magic Johnson – and there are many who believe he will develop in that mold. He is 6′ 8″ and can see over opposing defenses as he directs an offense. He also has a deadly three-point shot.

Don MacLean erased all the scoring records at UCLA set by Jabbar and Walton, and then rubbed out Sean Elliott's Pac-10 scoring record in his senior year. He is a natural power forward. His scoring average increased every year in college, and his quick ball release enables him to shoot while he is on the way up instead of waiting until he reaches the peak of his jump.

As these rising stars join the ranks of the NBA's greatest players, and as today's basketball heroes become tomorrow's legends, the NBA will continue to attract additional millions of fans here and abroad. The comings and goings of star players who make a difference – to their teams, their fans and in the record books – creates the colorful legacy of pro basketball. And that is what the NBA is about.

Below: *LSU star and 1992 NBA draft pick Shaquille O'Neal.*

Below right: *Jim Jackson gave up his last year at college to join the NBA.*

MICHAEL ADAMS

Position: Guard
College: Boston College
Drafted: Sacramento, 1st Rd. ('85)

Birth Date: Jan. 19, 1963
Height: 5′ 10″
Weight: 165

Michael Adams has made a mockery out of scouting reports that said, "He is too small to play."

The only problem is that it took him a long time to convince the pro basketball gurus that he could not only survive, but also succeed beyond their wildest dreams. It took stints in the NBA with Sacramento, Denver and twice with Washington, plus a season of minor league basketball, before he forced the pros to recognize his ability.

He has found his niche with his fine three-point shooting and his ability to run an offense.

Consider:

He is the NBA's all-time three-point scoring leader and while playing for Denver, he hit at least one three-pointer in a record 79 consecutive games.

In making the 1992 NBA All-Star team, he was second to Michael Jordan in the balloting for the "off-guard."

"He is all we want in a point guard," Bullets general manager John Nash says. "His points and leadership are outstanding, but his ability to go into the lane and cause havoc is a special ingredient."

Right: *Michael Adams (left), a 5′ 10″, 165-pound guard, has proven that there is a place for the "little guy" in the NBA. He's proven it with his outside shooting, quick drive to the basket and all-around ability as an "off," or shooting guard. In 1991 his 54 points against Milwaukee were the most by any NBA player in a single game that year, and he is the league's all-time three-point shooter. In 1992 he broke the Bullets' team record for three-point field goals.*

NICK ANDERSON

Right: Nick Anderson optioned to leave college a year early, then quickly transformed the fine rebounding and defensive skills he'd honed at the University of Illinois into a better all-around game in the NBA. He helped form the nucleus of an improving Orlando Magic team in the early nineties, and became a team scoring leader.

Position: Guard
College: Illinois
Drafted: Orlando, 1st Rd. ('89)

Birth Date: Jan. 20, 1968
Height: 6′ 6″
Weight: 215

Nick Anderson surprised many in the NBA when he opted to forego his final year of college eligibility at the University of Illinois and tossed his name into the 1989 draft. The Orlando Magic were delighted.

Within three seasons, Anderson became the Magic's go-to guy, and they have begun to build their future around him and Georgia Tech's Dennis Scott.

With his steady production climb and his solid all-around play, Anderson has fulfilled all that the Magic had hoped he could provide. For example, in his rookie season he averaged 11.5 points per game. But by his third year, he had tied for the club scoring leadership with a 19.9 points per game average.

He accumulated 316 rebounds as a rookie, 386 the next year and over 500 by his third season, while also throwing in more than 100 assists in each of those seasons. His defense also improved: he totaled 97 steals in his third season, compared to 69 as a rookie and 74 in his second year. With his fine athletic skills, he gained a reputation as a shot-blocker. As a junior in college he developed into a 54 percent field goal shooter, and also added 38 percent from three-point range.

Anderson is a powerfully-built player, reminding many of Clyde Drexler of the Portland Trail Blazers. That strength, combined with a "nose" for the ball, has helped with his rebounding.

"Nick's best years still are ahead of him," comments Orlando Magic coach Matt Goukas. "When he has a stronger team around him, he will be one of the elite players in the NBA."

CHARLES BARKLEY

Position: Forward   **Birth Date:** Feb. 20, 1963
College: Auburn   **Height:** 6′ 6″
Drafted: Philadelphia, 1st Rd. (’84) **Weight:** 252

Charles Barkley has never been at a loss for words – about himself, his team, your team, his owner and fans, and anything else that strikes his fancy.

He also has never been found wanting on the basketball court, where he presents an awesome sight as he comes roaring down the floor, looking all the while like a rhino out of control. And that is how defenders in the NBA treat him – deliberately staying out of his way when he is cruising into the basket.

Barkley is one of the most unusual players in the sport's history, and not because of his size. But it is his size that calls attention to all that he does. "No one in the game is stronger," says Kevin McHale of the Boston Celtics, who has waged some classic battles against Barkley for over a half dozen seasons. "He takes up so much space that you really can't knock him out of the way, much less think about knocking him off the ball. Instead, it is the other way around. You think you have the board covered and all of a sudden Charles roars in and you wonder what happened."

Barkley looks more like a pro football lineman than an NBA forward, yet he has the grace and athleticism of a player 30 or 40 pounds lighter, and a few inches smaller. His size causes teams tremendous problems in trying to match up.

Unlike some very big players whose main job is to clog the middle and try to keep opposing rebounders away, Barkley has a deft shooting touch. Before being

Left: *Charles Barkley is one of the NBA's most colorful players, who backs up much of his outrageousness with some great playing skills that earned him four straight selections to the All-NBA team from 1988 to 1991, and the MVP Award in the 1991 All-Star Game.*

Opposite: *Barkley is quick enough to go one-on-one with opposing forwards, and has averaged 23 points a game during his career. "I know how to play the game," commented the confident Barkley. "You can't fool me. I might make a mistake, but I know what it takes to be successful, and I know who can play and who can't."*

Opposite, inset: *After being cut during trials for the 1984 U.S. Olympic team, Barkley joined Chris Mullin (left) and David Robinson (right) on the 1992 team.*

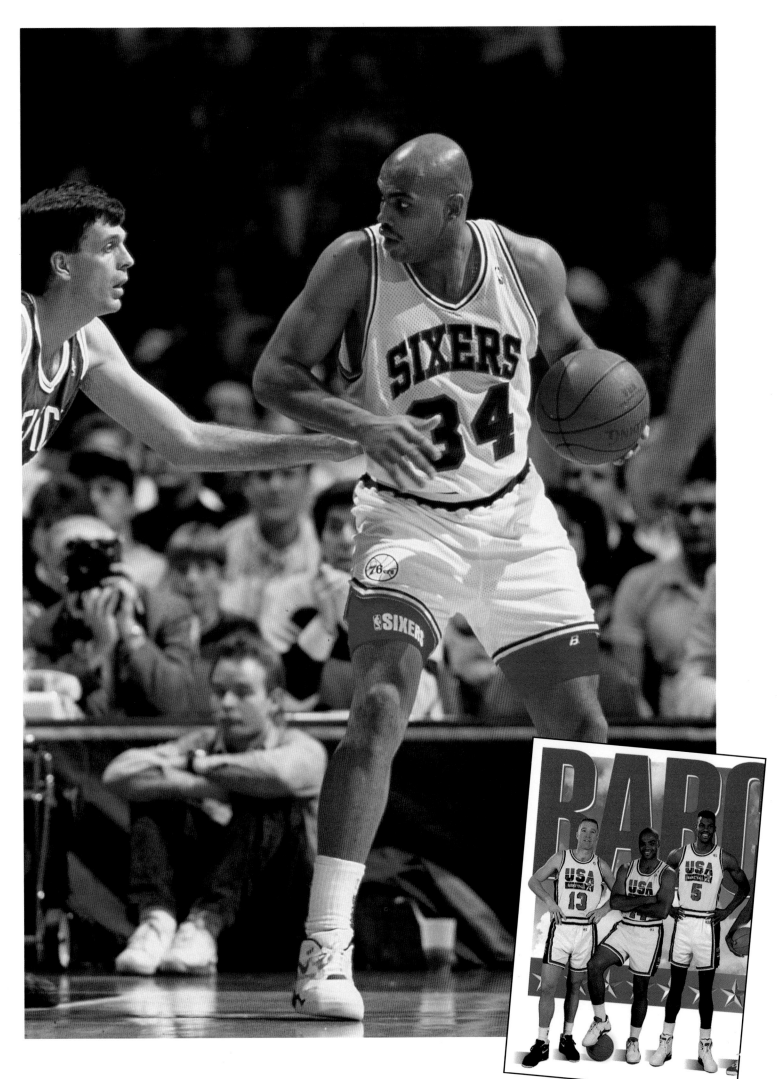

Opposite: *To complement his scoring ability, Barkley averages almost 12 rebounds per game.*

Above: *At 6' 6" and 252 pounds, Barkley is a fearsome sight rumbling down the court.*

them up against anybody's."

He has been a regular on the NBA All-Star team, and he was selected as the game's MVP in 1991 after pulling down 22 rebounds – the most since Wilt Chamberlain's performance in the 1967 game.

Barkley was the fourth all-time scorer at Auburn when he left a year early to play pro ball, and was later picked as the Southeast Conference's Player of the Decade of the Eighties. He was cut by coach Bobby Knight late in the 1984 U.S. Olympic trials ("he did me a great favor because I found out what it takes to compete at a higher level"), but was named to America's team for the 1992 games at Barcelona.

traded to Phoenix after the 1992 season, he ranked in the top five among all-time 76ers scorers, and led his team in six of his first seven NBA seasons.

He is the biggest "small forward" in the NBA, and has become a force around the boards with his rebounds, averaging more than 800 per season.

"The key to rebounding is your legs and I have supreme confidence in my legs," Barkley says. "I'll put

DEE BROWN

Position: Guard   **Birth Date:** Nov. 29, 1968
College: Jacksonville University   **Height:** 6′ 1″
Drafted: Boston, 1st Rd. ('90)   **Weight:** 160

Dee Brown stunned the NBA's entertainment establishment when he won the Slam Dunk contest as a rookie in 1991. He shook them up even more when he made the NBA's all-rookie team three months later after his first season with the Boston Celtics. A 6′ 1″ rookie wasn't supposed to come in and dethrone not only all the hot dog slam dunkers, but more acclaimed stars with All-America credentials. Dee Brown had quickly become a household – or at least, playground – hero of sorts.

Part of his charm was that Brown came into a big man's game with a little man's credentials – with an unimpressive height and a scrawny 160 pounds. But within that tightly wrapped frame are natural coils that enable him to do some amazing things on a basketball court. If anyone had paid attention when he played college basketball, they would have known that, as Jacksonville University's best rebounder, Dee "played" about a half foot taller than he really was.

But even the Celtics were skeptical – or not too interested – until Dee starred in a pre-draft all-star game in Orlando, Florida, where he eclipsed far more touted stars. After the Boston Celtics drafted him in 1990, they made him point guard, giving him responsibility to run their offense. He did it so well as a rookie that they traded their 1989 number one draft pick, Brian Shaw, who had done that job with some distinction for a couple of seasons.

DERRICK COLEMAN

Position: Forward
College: Syracuse
Drafted: New Jersey, 1st Rd. ('90)

Birth Date: June 21, 1967
Height: 6′ 10″
Weight: 230

Derrick Coleman was a collegiate legend when he came into the NBA as its first pick of the 1990 draft.

As a four-year starter at Syracuse, he became the NCAA's all-time rebound leader with a total of 1,537; and he is recognized as the first player ever to score 2,000 points, grab 1,500 rebounds and block 300 shots in a career.

Coleman has begun to live up to those figures in the pros. He certainly underscored his first-draft selection honor by being named Rookie of the Year for 1991, after being New Jersey's number two scorer that season, with 1,364 points. He led the team in scoring 26 times. He recorded 40 double-doubles that year, and led the Nets in rebounding.

As befits a great player, Coleman can rise to the occasion against another great player. For example, against former Syracuse teammate Ron Seikaly of the Miami Heat, one of the NBA's top rebounding centers, he hit his 1992 season high with 38 points in 39 minutes, adding seven rebounds and three assists.

Opposite: *Though just 6′ 1″, Dee Brown often played as a forward at Jacksonville University because of his great rebounding ability. That's one of the reasons the Celtics made him a surprise number one draft pick in 1991. He proved his worth by being named to the NBA all-rookie team after also winning the NBA's Slam Dunk Contest.*

Right: *Derrick Coleman was the first player chosen in the 1990 player draft by the New Jersey Nets after an All-America season at Syracuse. He won NBA Rookie of the Year honors after averaging more than 18 points per game, and pulling down 759 rebounds. He also is an able three-point field goal shooter.*

BRAD DAUGHERTY

Position: Center   **Birth Date:** Oct. 19, 1965
College: North Carolina   **Height:** 7′ 0″
Drafted: Cleveland, 1st Rd. (’86)   **Weight:** 263

For years, no one gave the Cleveland Cavaliers much respect because they had one mediocre season after another.

But all of that began to change in 1986 when the Cavs, with the first pick in the draft, selected All-America center Brad Daugherty from North Carolina. Gradually, with some solid coaching by Len Wilkins and with help from a bevy of good role players who took on some of the burdens, Daugherty became one of the game’s best players, and the Cavaliers became contenders.

“Everyone revolves around him,” says a teammate, “but he doesn’t have to be in control. We just focus on what he does and then add our own talent.”

18

Opposite top: *Brad Daugherty has led the Cleveland Cavaliers in rebounding every season he's been with them except 1990, when he missed half the games with an injury.*

Opposite below: *Daugherty was the first draft pick of Cleveland – and the NBA – after an All-America season at North Carolina in 1986. He was named to the 1987 NBA all-rookie team.*

Right: *Despite his great size and strength, at 7' and 263 pounds, Daugherty has a deft shooting touch and has always been first or second in field goal shooting percentage for the Cavaliers, except in an injury-shortened 1990 season.*

That is important. The Cavs are a total package offense and Daugherty's play often fits so snugly into that package that his contributions occur without fanfare. Yet, in a 33-game stretch during the 1991-92 season, he outscored the opposing center 29 times – and five of those centers included future Hall of Famers Patrick Ewing, Robert Parish, Hakeem Olajuwon, David Robinson and Moses Malone.

It has been work to reach that level, and he still is growing as a player. "The key is constant application of my skills, something that took a while for me to learn," Daugherty says.

Those skills are a blend of finesse and strength. Though he is seven feet tall, he did not come into the NBA and tear up the boards. He never has been among the NBA's great shot-blockers and his rebounding skills have inched up each year to the point where he now is among the top five centers in the league.

Yet, no center can match his fine shooting touch. He can hit right-handed hooks from either side of the lane,

or run the center of the fast break and stop and pop a feathery shot from 15 feet out. He can back down to the basket on a dribble and then loft a soft shot while other big centers mostly power their way to the hoop and slam dunk the ball. Daugherty can do that too, and with all of the thunder you'd expect from someone who is seven feet tall, and 263 pounds. But he has the knack of using his array of shots at the right time.

This all-around ballhandling skill, coupled with his ability to see the entire floor and distribute the ball, makes double-teaming him a risky proposition.

One of the less discernible assets is his great strength. "I grew up getting stepped on by bulls when I worked on my family's farm," he says. "I had to carry my share of a heavy load of farm work. I'm as strong as any player in the league, but people often mistake the gentle side of my nature for weakness. I don't take anything off anybody, and if you come to play me, I'm going to try and kick your butt. I may not always do it, but I'm going to try."

VLADE DIVAC

Left: *Vlade Divac is the latest in a succession of great Lakers centers that includes George Mikan, Wilt Chamberlain and Kareem Abdul-Jabbar. Considered one of the best European players in the late eighties, he helped his native Yugoslavia win a silver medal in the 1988 Olympic Games. Divac adjusted brilliantly to playing in the NBA, where the opposition's talent level is tougher, and there are more games than in European basketball.*

Position: Center   **Birth Date:** Feb. 3, 1968
College: None   **Height:** 7' 1"
Drafted: L.A. Lakers, 1st Rd. ('89)   **Weight:** 250

Vlade Divac didn't have to learn about hero worship in the NBA. He was an established star in his native Yugoslavia long before he came to the U.S., having played the game on a professional level since he was 16 years old.

But he had never had to fill two of pro basketball's biggest shoes – those belonging to Kareem Abdul-Jabbar, the highest scoring and rebounding center in NBA history. Divac was thrust into that role after being a first-round pick in 1989, and the Lakers believe he is on the way to carving out his own niche at that

position; in 1992, they gave him an $18 million contract that runs for most of the nineties.

When Divac joined the Lakers in 1989, no one knew whether he could adjust to the language, culture and style of NBA basketball, and still meld with a team that had such established stars as Magic Johnson and James Worthy. Divac earned his money by coping with the pressure of succeeding Jabbar. For one thing, he brought a different personality – outgoing, gregarious and mischievous – that contrasted to the often-moody Jabbar.

On the court, he helped the team into the NBA finals in 1991, his second season and first as full-time starter. In 1992 he recovered from serious back surgery and helped the Lakers back into another playoff spot.

CLYDE DREXLER

Position: Guard   **Birth Date:** June 22, 1962
College: University of Houston   **Height:** 6′ 7″
Drafted: Portland, 1st Rd. ('83)   **Weight:** 222

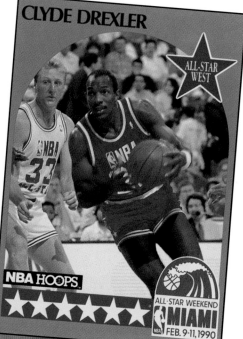

Many in the NBA claim that if Clyde Drexler played in New York, Los Angeles or Chicago, he would be among the league's five most popular players. Instead, he plays in Portland, Oregon, the NBA's smallest market, and those fans love him madly.

He is the team's all-time leader in eight of 10 major statistical areas (all but three-point shots attempted and made), a perennial All-Star Game participant and the go-to guy when things are tough. In short, he is the principal reason why the Trail Blazers became a force in the Western Division early in the 1990s.

Drexler came into the NBA with some good credentials – a member of the University of Houston's rollicking "Phi Slama Jama" teams that made racehorse basketball a way of life en route to consecutive trips to

Above: *Drexler has been named to a half dozen NBA All-Star teams and has led his Portland team to the playoffs during his first eight NBA seasons.*

Left: *Clyde Drexler was named to the 1992 U.S. Olympic team after leading the 1992 Portland Trail Blazers in scoring, assists and steals.*

the NCAA Final Four.

Those credentials and his athleticism were impressive, but when he came into the NBA some believed him to be an incomplete player, questioning his passing and ballhandling skills, his outside shooting and his durability. His Blazer teammates looked to him for offense, and that mainly consisted of his ability to drive to the basket. But when Drexler refined his outside shooting, it became a perfect foil against defenders overplaying his drives. Then, as the club improved, the scoring load was more evenly distributed and his assists and rebounds increased. The quintessential team player was in his element.

He thrives on pressure because self-confidence never has been a problem for him. "If you don't believe in yourself, who else is going to believe in you?" he asks. "Sure, there's a fine line. You don't want to be arrogant or cocky, but you have to have a quiet belief in yourself."

In Portland, that belief is a bit more than quiet.

Opposite: *Clyde Drexler was a member of the University of Houston's "Phi Slama Jama" team that played in two NCAA Final Fours, and he was the first Cougars player to accumulate 1,000 points, 900 rebounds and 300 assists.*

Above right: *No guard in the NBA is faster afoot than Drexler, who is renowned for his explosive end-to-end drives. He is often compared to Michael Jordan with his driving, swooping style of offensive play, something he considers the supreme compliment, though he commented, "I don't compete against Michael and I don't play for recognition. What I can do for Portland is all that matters."*

Right: *Clyde Drexler participates in the 1992 All-Star Game. Drexler's game has grown to the point where, though playing guard, he has accumulated more rebounds than assists. He is the Trail Blazers' all-time leader in eight of 10 major statistics.*

Page 26: *Drexler battles Magic Johnson in the 1991 Western Conference finals, but they worked for a common cause as teammates on the 1992 U.S. Olympic team.*

JOE DUMARS

Position: Guard
College: McNeese State
Drafted: Detroit, 1st Rd. ('85)

Birth Date: May 24, 1963
Height: 6′ 3″
Weight: 190

When the Detroit Pistons were among the NBA's elite in the late eighties and early nineties – culminating with back-to-back titles in 1989 and 1990 – their most underrated player was guard Joe Dumars. He also was their most valuable player.

Even with the Pistons' halcyon championship years apparently behind them, Dumars continues to apply leadership and consistent production. He was selected as MVP in Detroit's first world championship victory; received a fair bit of notoriety when named to three consecutive NBA All-Star teams in 1990, '91 and '92; and led the team in scoring in both the 1991 and 1992 seasons. More important to him was his first team selection to the league's all-defensive team in 1989 and 1990.

"Fans probably were never aware of what Joe really was doing until the game was over and everything fell into place," noted former Detroit coach Chuck Daly. "We never judged his performances by boxscore numbers, but he was like the glue that held us together in tough spots. . . . Joe was steady, unrelenting, and when we asked him to take on the other team's big scoring guard, he always gave us a good game."

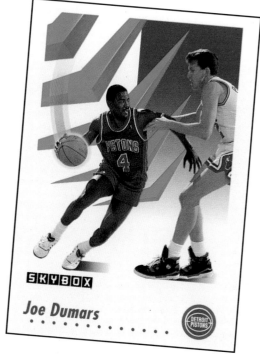

Joe Dumars

SKYBOX

Above: *Joe Dumars played on two Detroit NBA championship teams in 1989-90, and was playoff MVP in 1989.*

Below: *Dumars was twice named to the NBA's All-Defensive team, and twice led Detroit in scoring.*

SEAN ELLIOTT

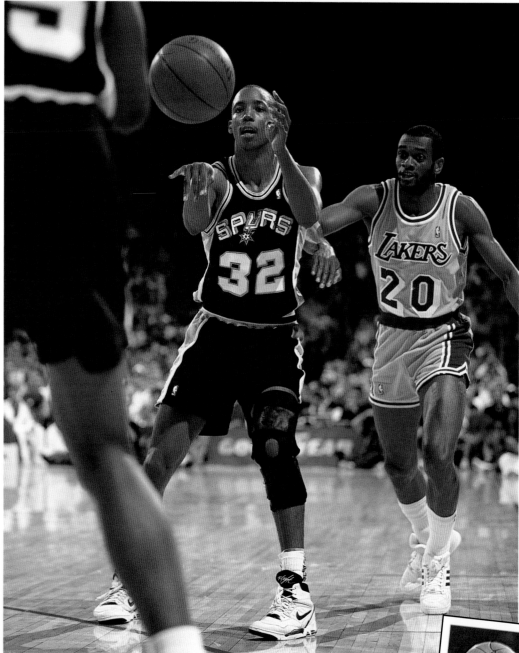

Left: *Sean Elliott was the third player selected in the 1989 draft as a lottery pick by San Antonio, after playing four seasons at the University of Arizona where he finished as the Pac-10's all-time scorer.*

Below: *Elliott's team wins nearly 75 percent of its games when he scores 20 or more points. He also led the Spurs in foul shooting accuracy in each of his first three seasons. His defensive contribution was evident in the 1991 playoffs. After an injury forced Elliott to leave a game early in the second half, Golden State's Chris Mullin – whom Elliott had held to just six points – went wild and scored 21 of his 27 points.*

Position: Forward   **Birth Date:** Feb. 2, 1968
College: Arizona   **Height:** 6' 8"
Drafted: San Antonio, 1st Rd. ('89)   **Weight:** 215

Sean Elliott has a clear view of his role with the San Antonio Spurs: "Our big guns have always been Terry Cummings and David Robinson and I am just there to support them. If either one isn't on, I'm fully capable of picking it up."

And how. The 6' 8" forward has become a major force in the Spurs' offense, but more importantly, a great contributor on defense.

Elliott had made the same contributions during two All-America seasons at the University of Arizona, where he led the Wildcats to the Final Four in his junior season. As a senior, he finished as the PAC-10's all-time scorer, breaking the record set by center Lew Alcindor. He was chosen college basketball's Player of the Year by the Associated Press.

PERVIS ELLISON

Position: Center
College: Louisville
Drafted: Sacramento, 1st Rd ('89)

Birth Date: April 3, 1967
Height: 6' 10"
Weight: 225

Above left: *Pervis Ellison was the NBA's No. 1 draft pick in 1989.*

Above: *Ellison was traded by Sacramento to Washington in 1990.*

"Never Nervous" Pervis was a player from whom great things were immediately expected. As a freshman, he was the MVP of the 1986 NCAA Final Four and led Louisville to the collegiate championship in the final game against Duke. Sacramento made him the very first pick of the 1989 draft, but he was stymied for two years by injuries and a belief that he was not dedicated to the game.

But being traded to the Bullets in 1990, and his ability to work with coach Wes Unseld, has helped Ellison realize his potential.

First, Unseld brought him off the bench for much of his first season in Washington and alleviated a lot of self-imposed pressure. Then, he began to pound home the fine points of the game – and worked to toughen his mind. Ellison's improved attitude complemented some marvelous basketball skills, foremost being his ability to leap. He once leapt six inches shy of touching the top of the backboard. This, and a quick "second jump" ability, help his rebounding.

"I'm not trying to bang with bigger guys inside because I am not strong enough to play them even-up," says Ellison, whose weight loss during a season brings him close to 200 pounds. "I'm using my quickness to beat them to the hole."

Jerry Reynolds of the Sacramento Kings best summarized his skills when, after Ellison had topped a poll of "most improved players" in 1991, noted: "We always thought he was a player. We shouldn't have done the deal."

PATRICK EWING

Position: Center   **Birth Date:** Aug. 5, 1962
College: Georgetown   **Height:** 7′ 0″
Drafted: New York, 1st Rd. ('85)   **Weight:** 240

"Do what it takes to win." That is the first and foremost commandment in Patrick Ewing's lexicon of basic basketball rules. And since entering the NBA as the first "lottery" pick in 1985, he has tried valiantly to adhere to that idea.

It hasn't always been easy because the Knicks went through six coaches in Ewing's first seven seasons, and the stability that any player needs – even great ones like him – sapped his ability to help produce championships.

Still, there is no more dominating center in the NBA than the seven-foot native of Jamaica who was a schoolboy sensation in Cambridge, Massachusetts, and who attracted scholarship offers from over 300 colleges. He chose Georgetown University in Washington, and led the Hoyas to three appearances in the NCAA championship game.

While in college, he also helped lead the United States to the gold medal in the 1984 Olympic Games.

So coveted were his talents – and so worried were NBA officials about what clubs might do to get them – that they devised a "lottery pick" system in 1985 for teams not making the playoffs to determine their first-

Above: Patrick Ewing was the No. 1 draft pick in the NBA in 1985 by the New York Knicks and has been the team's starting center since the first game of his pro career.

Right: Ewing is the only Knick ever to score 2,000 points in more than one season, and led the Knicks in scoring in each of his first seven seasons. Renowned for his thunderous dunks, he has learned how to control his game, and blend his scoring and his defense into one package.

Opposite: In college Ewing played in three NCAA championship games, helping his Georgetown team to the title in 1984. As a collegian he also won a gold medal with the 1984 U.S. Olympic team. Ewing was a member of the 1992 U.S. Olympic team as well.

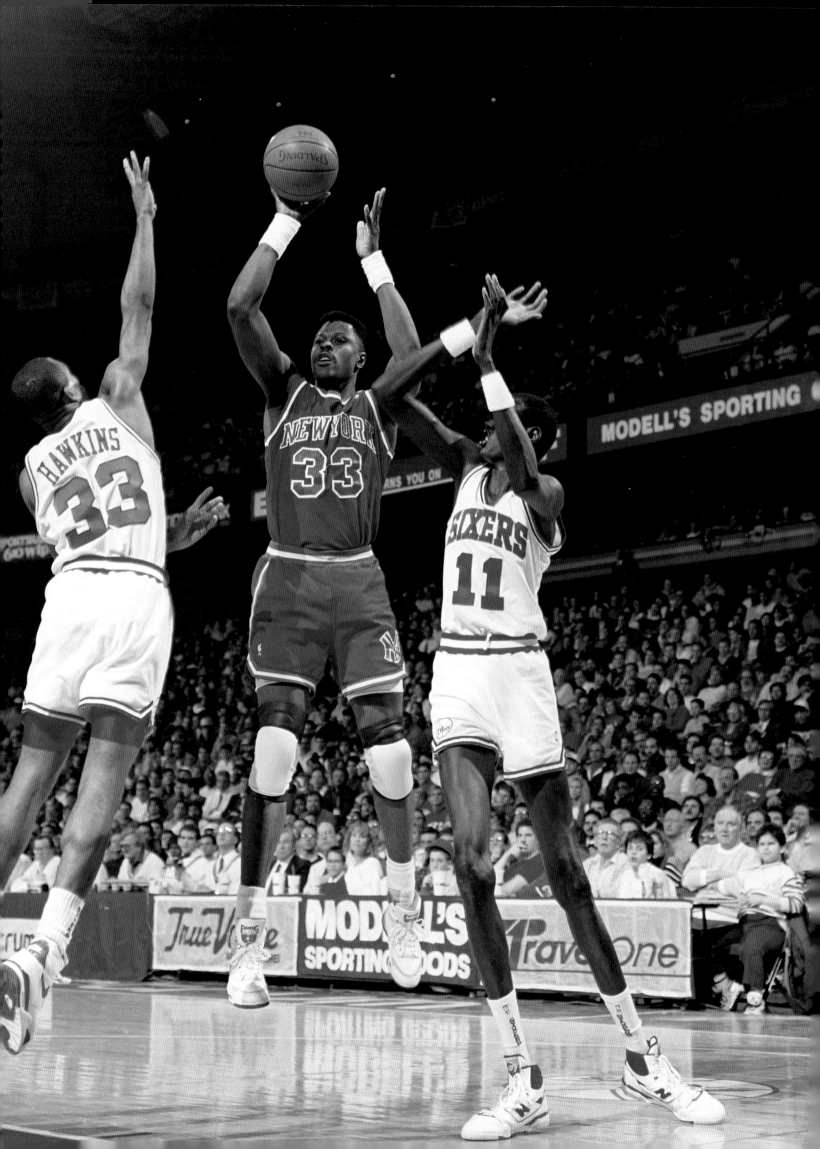

round selection position. The New York Knicks came up with the top pick that year and they chose Ewing.

The NBA couldn't have been happier to have its newest superstar playing in the nation's largest city with all of the attendant media. But with all that exposure also came tremendous pressure on this young giant. Though he was chosen the NBA's Rookie of the Year in 1986 and was the only rookie named to the All-Star team that year, he became a lightning rod for critics who had bought the idea that he was the "next" Bill Russell. Ewing, who had been tutored by Russell, had displayed some of those skills as a collegian. "He had an ability to coil and recoil on blocked shots, swatting one attempt away, and then recovering to go after another," said Dave Gavitt, former Big East commissioner. "We haven't seen that since Bill Russell."

So the comparisons were too easily tossed around when he entered the pros. Ewing responded in part by becoming the team's all-time blocked-shot leader, and the first Knicks player ever to have two 2,000-point seasons.

Sometimes his game-controlling offense can be an awesome sight. For example, during one stretch of the 1992 season, he scored his team's final six points in the last 61 seconds of a game against Dallas, getting the game-winner with six seconds to play. Ten days later, against Detroit, he capped a 45-point performance with a fall-away jump shot with 20 seconds to play for the winning basket; and two days after that, he scored six straight points in the final two minutes to wipe out a four-point Charlotte lead in a Knicks' victory.

"I've never been out to copy anyone's style," says the ambitious Patrick Ewing. "I just want to be known as one of the best ever."

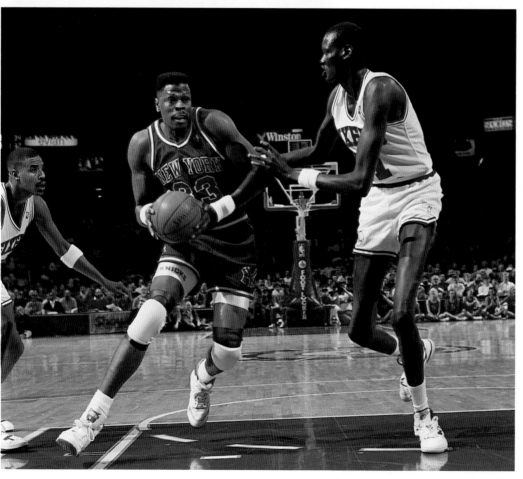

Above left: *Patrick Ewing with All-Star rival Hakeem Olajuwon in 1988. Ewing has played in a half-dozen NBA All-Star Games.*

Left: *Ewing set a club record with 2,347 points in 1990, and he was the only player that year to rank among the NBA's top six in scoring, rebounding, blocked shots and shooting average.*

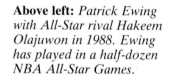

Opposite: *Ewing is the fifth player in the Knicks' history to score 10,000 points, and was New York's second leading all-time scorer after just seven seasons. He also has scored 50 points in a game twice during his career.*

HORACE GRANT

Position: Forward   **Birth Date:** July 4, 1965
College: Clemson   **Height:** 6' 10"
Drafted: Chicago, 1st Rd. ('87)   **Weight:** 220

In a move to surround their talented Michael Jordan with better players, the Bulls chose Horace Grant with the 10th pick on the first round in 1987, and traded for Scottie Pippen on the same day. Four years later, the Bulls – with Jordan, Grant and Pippen – won the first of two straight NBA world championships.

Grant has supplied the much-needed up-front muscle as the Bulls' power forward, and relieved Jordan from some of the heavy defensive duties.

"Horace doesn't get the notoriety that Michael and Scottie receive because he is not a featured offensive player," notes coach Phil Jackson. "We asked him to hit the boards, help our center, and allow the other two guys to do their thing, and he responded as well as we ever could have hoped."

The Bulls consider him on a par with the NBA's best power forwards. And they have the championship rings to prove it.

Left: The Chicago Bulls did not contend seriously for an NBA title until Horace Grant became power forward after being a first-round draft pick in 1987. His twin brother, Harvey, was a first-round pick by Washington a year later. Horace Grant was Chicago's leading rebounder for his first four seasons.

TIM HARDAWAY

Position: Guard   **Birth Date:** Sept. 1, 1966
College: U Texas-El Paso   **Height:** 6′ 0″
Drafted: Golden State, 1st Rd. ('89)   **Weight:** 170

Tim Hardaway has not had an easy time becoming one of the premier point guards in the NBA. He was downgraded as a pro prospect because of his size, lack of top competition and erratic shooting – except by coach Don Nelson of the Golden State Warriors. "Everytime we saw him shoot, the ball went in," Nelson said, "and we couldn't believe our good fortune when he still was available on the 14th pick of the first round in 1989. We figured he'd be gone by the fourth pick."

Even as a rookie, his crossover move to the hoop bamboozled the most experienced NBA guards. His weakness was shooting from the outside. So in his first off-season, he shot 300 to 500 balls every day, and in his second year he offered two bad choices to opponents: Play him tight and be victimized by the quick crossover move to the basket; play loose to cut off that move and be nailed by the outside jumper.

Above: *Tim Hardaway was a unanimous selection to the NBA's all-rookie team in 1990 after averaging 14.7 points per game.*

Right: *Hardaway was the youngest player, at 24, in the 1991 NBA All-Star Game, where he scored five points in 12 minutes.*

During those first two seasons, he also established himself as a brash, cocky, trash-talker who backed down from no one. His scoring average went from 14.7 per game as a rookie, to 22.9 and his first All-Star Game in his second season. He was there again in 1992, scoring 14 points, including a pair of three-pointers in five tries that were launched with his typical flourish.

"I expect to be in this game for many years to come," he said afterward. "I have worked to be chosen as one of the best at my position in the NBA and I am just going to be me whenever I play."

Coach Nelson believes his team developed a more physical, competitive style since Hardaway joined them. The Warriors love his play as point guard, which is a natural position for him with his instinctive, fiery leadership, adroit ballhandling and now, good outside shooting. "The throne is his if he wants it," says Magic Johnson, considered the premier point guard of the eighties (and by some, of all time).

To which Nelson added: "He will be one of the top four or five point guards for as long as he's in the NBA."

Opposite: *Hardaway accumulated over 2,000 assists in his first three seasons at Golden State, and also averaged more than 20 points per game.*

Above: *Tim is a fiery competitor and received the team's McMahon Award as its most inspirational player when he was a rookie.*

Left: *Hardaway wore No. 5 when he first joined Golden State instead of the No. 10 that he had at U Texas-El Paso where he broke Tiny Archibald's scoring records. He reclaimed No. 10 after center Manute Bol left Golden State.*

Page 38: *Hardaway drives to the basket. With his physical playing style, his deft ballhandling skills and his crossover move to the hoop, Hardaway is one of the NBA's best point guards.*

DEREK HARPER

Left: *A national publication rated Derek Harper as the "NBA's best guard defending on the ball" and he backed it up by becoming the Dallas Mavericks' all-time steals leader. He was also the only Dallas player ever to have been selected to the NBA's All-Defensive teams.*

Below: *Harper was the first player in NBA history to increase his scoring average in each of his first eight seasons. A prolific three-point shooter, he set a club record in 1990 by hitting at least one three-pointer in 12 consecutive games.*

Position: Guard   **Birth Date:** Oct. 13, 1961
College: Illinois   **Height:** 6′ 4″
Drafted: Dallas, 1st Rd. ('83)   **Weight:** 200

Derek Harper's greatest personal delight is swiping the ball away from a point guard and turning the play into a score – and it didn't take him very long to establish the Dallas Mavericks' career record for steals.

"That's my main thing," says Harper. "I think I've been given the label around the league as being one of the best defensive players."

Not that his offense is bad; each season he also has been among his team's top scorers and assist-makers. "But the simple fact is that you don't always shoot the ball well," he says. "Defense can win games."

"His defense really helps his offense, particularly with his ability to steal the ball," observes Magic Johnson, who is second in the NBA's all-time steals department and believes that Harper will surpass his own career totals.

RON HARPER

Position: Guard   **Birth Date:** Jan. 20, 1964
College: Miami (Ohio)   **Height:** 6′ 6″
Drafted: Cleveland, 1st Rd. ('86)   **Weight:** 198

The Cleveland Cavaliers traded Ron Harper, plus first-round draft picks in 1990 and 1991, and a second-round pick in 1992, to the Los Angeles Clippers in exchange for the rights to former Duke All-America Danny Ferry and guard Reggie Williams. That was too much, the skeptics claimed.

Harper proved his value when he helped pick up the lowly Clippers and move them into the playoffs for the first time ever in 1992, just as he had helped the Cavaliers to the second best record in the NBA in '89.

Harper has thrived with the coming of Larry Brown as coach of the Clippers because he has been able to play the kind of game that suits his talents – an "in the paint" offense instead of standing around and bombing away with low percentage three-point shots.

"This is the same slashing style of offense that I used so successfully with Cleveland, and one in which I am not only more comfortable, but obviously more effective," Harper said.

Harper made a fine recovery after tearing the ligaments in his right knee early in the 1990 season. Until the injury that season, the Clippers were 14-14; afterward, they were 14-33, and for the entire 80 games that he missed, the team was 28-60. He then played the entire 1992 season and the Clippers went to the playoffs.

That's being valuable.

HERSEY HAWKINS

Position: Guard
College: Bradley
Drafted: L.A. Clippers, 1st Rd. ('88)

Birth Date: Sept. 29, 1965
Height: 6′ 3″
Weight: 190

Hersey Hawkins's NBA career was played in the huge shadow of Charles Barkley. But with Barkley gone, he can enlarge his own niche as a play-maker and three-point shooter-par excellence.

The 76ers traded for him on draft day in 1988 after he was selected as the sixth pick of the first round by the L.A. Clippers. To get Hawkins, Philadelphia sent Charles Smith, whom they selected with the third pick in the first round, and a 1989 first-round pick, to L.A. Coming to Philadelphia was the culmination of a dream of sorts for Hawkins, whose favorite player while growing up was 76ers great, Julius Erving. Thrust into the starting lineup, Hawkins made his mark by being named to the NBA's all-rookie first team. He also scored 1,196 points, the most ever by a 76ers rookie.

He graduated from the all-rookie team to the NBA All-Star team in his third season. Hersey also is the 76ers' all-time leader in three-point field goals, and he holds the club's season record in that department.

As a collegian, Hawkins was an All-America player at Bradley University in Peoria, Illinois, where he was a near-unanimous selection as Player of the Year. He also was the nation's leading collegiate scorer that year and finished his career fourth on the all-time list.

Hawkins was a member of the U.S. Olympic team in 1988, and an injury that forced him from the game against the USSR probably cost the Americans a chance to win the gold medal.

Opposite top: *Ron Harper was a unanimous choice for the 1987 NBA all-rookie team, and runner-up in Rookie of the Year voting while playing with the Cleveland Cavaliers. The Cavs traded him to the Los Angeles Clippers in 1989.*

Opposite bottom: *Major knee surgery in 1990 cost Harper parts of two seasons but did not dull his slashing, attacking style of offense. After coach Larry Brown joined the Clippers in 1992, Harper began operating closer to the basket, and improved his shooting percentage from 39 to 51 percent.*

Right: *Hersey Hawkins is a prolific scorer, and often outscored teammate Charles Barkley, while setting a 76ers' club record with 108 three-pointers in 1990. He also led the team in steals in both the 1991 and 1992 seasons.*

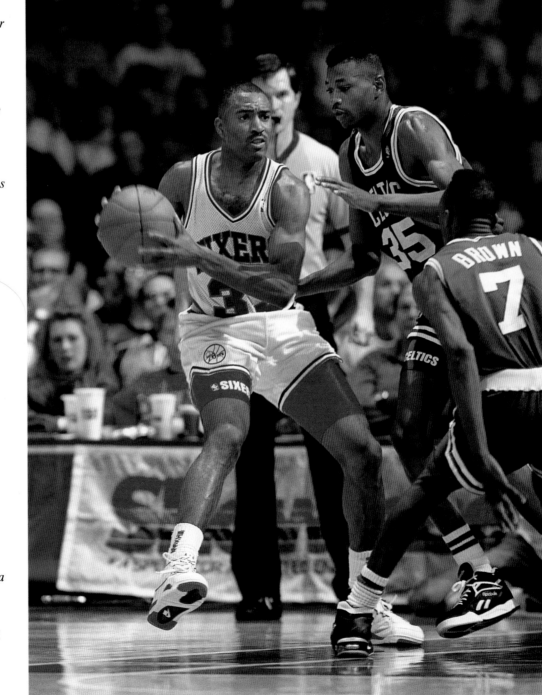

JEFF HORNACEK

Position: Guard **Birth Date:** May 3, 1963
College: Iowa State **Height:** 6' 4"
Drafted: Phoenix, 2nd Rd. ('86) **Weight:** 190

Jeff Hornacek makes the "fine wine" team – he just keeps getting better with age.

Hornacek led the Phoenix Suns in scoring in 1992, his sixth season – and that's not bad considering that in his rookie year, he was 11th with a 5.5 points per game average. In 1992 he averaged 20 points. He was traded to Philadelphia after the season in a deal that brought Charles Barkley to Phoenix.

Hornacek was among Phoenix' top five in free throws, shooting, assists and steals; and he finished first in each of those categories in at least one season. All of this has helped him to four All-Star Games.

What made his achievements even more startling was sharing the backcourt with another NBA All-Star, Kevin Johnson, whose talents mirrored his own.

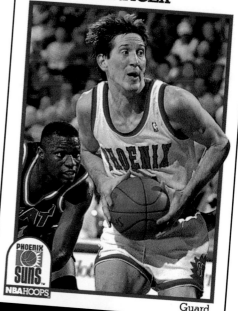

Guard

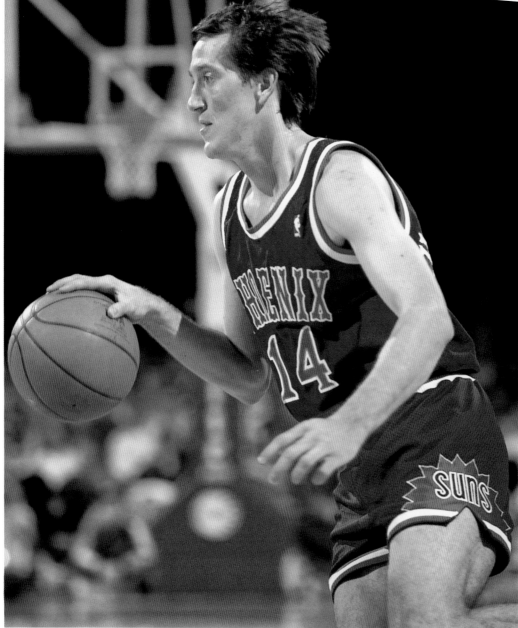

Above: *Jeff Hornacek is renowned for his playmaking, beginning with his rookie season with Phoenix when he set team records of 13 assists in a half, and 10 in a quarter. During his college years at Iowa State, Hornacek was only the second Big Eight player ever to accumulate more than 1,000 points and 600 assists; and his 665 total assists were a Big Eight career record.*

Left: *Hornacek is a fine three-point shooter and set a Phoenix Suns' record in 1991 when he hit five in one half. He also led the team in steals in three seasons, and was second twice, during his first six NBA seasons. He now brings those talents to Philadelphia.*

JAY HUMPHRIES

Position: Guard   **Birth Date:** Oct. 17, 1962
College: Colorado   **Height:** 6′ 3″
Drafted: Phoenix, 1st Rd. ('84)   **Weight:** 195

"I do what it takes to win games," says Jay Humphries, describing his playing style. "Everybody likes to score and get assists because those are the columns everybody looks at. But you can do other things on the court that are taken for granted, that only people really in the know understand."

To Humphries, that means concentrating on an all-around game, though he really is at home when distributing the ball to his teammates – and taking it away from the opposition. Since coming into the NBA as a number one draft pick of the Phoenix Suns in 1984, he was either first or second in assists and steals (he was third one season in the latter category) with both the Suns and Milwaukee Bucks. He was traded to Utah after the 1992 season.

Above: *Jay Humphries, one of the NBA's best point guards, led the Milwaukee Bucks in assists in four consecutive seasons, and also led Phoenix in two others. He has accumulated nearly 4,000 assists during his NBA career, averaging more than seven assists in every game he has started. Noted Del Harris, his former coach at Milwaukee, "I think it's important to be a leader and knowledgeable and to be unselfish, and Jay has developed his game along those lines."*

Right: *Even with his great flair for directing an offense, Humphries's all-around game was so important to the Bucks during the 1991 season that they won nine of the 13 games in which he also was the top scorer. In the NBA, the durable guard has averaged 78 games a year and more than 31 minutes per game.*

KEVIN JOHNSON

Position: Guard   **Birth Date:** March 6, 1966
College: U Cal-Berkeley   **Height:** 6′ 1″
Drafted: Cleveland, 1st Rd. (′87)   **Weight:** 190

What kind of a player is Kevin Johnson? He has been selected to the All-NBA team several times, made appearances in the All-Star Game, and is considered one of the NBA's best all-around guards.

But midway through the 1992 season, his Phoenix Suns coach, Cotton Fitzsimmons, chided him for being too unselfish.

Fitzsimmons's point was that Johnson was concentrating too much on spreading the ball around and bypassing open shots at a time when the team was missing its big scoring forward, Tom Chambers.

"If you'd taken five or six more shots, do you think we would have lost?" Fitzsimmons asked his All-Star guard after the Suns had lost by two points to Portland.

Fitzsimmons even commended Johnson for playing "a solid game," and told him how nice it was that he was getting everyone involved with his playmaking. "But," he added, "you're not taking your jump shot enough and we're not scoring enough points to win. I want you to be a shooter first, a playmaker second."

He said this to a player who has led the team in assists for each of his first four full seasons in Phoenix after coming to the Suns in a monster trade with the Cleve-

Above: *Kevin Johnson cost the Suns a bundle when they obtained him from the Cleveland Cavaliers, but he has been a perennial member of the NBA's post-season all-star teams.*

Left: *Johnson has often led the club in scoring and assists, and (**Opposite**) he is at his best when he takes his offense directly at the opposition.*

Page 46: *Johnson is an equal opportunity competitor and he has a reputation for battling everyone, even the NBA's big men such as 7′ 1″ Vlade Divac of the Los Angeles Lakers.*

land Cavaliers. The Suns sent Larry Nance, Mike Sanders and a 1992 second-round pick to Cleveland for Johnson, Mark West, Tyrone Corbin, first- and second-round draft picks in 1988 and a second-round pick in 1989.

Obviously, the Cavaliers were after Nance, and dismissed the potential of Johnson, though he was a number one pick that season. He left the University of California at Berkeley as the school's all-time scorer, assist-maker and leader in steals.

Kevin is a slashing driver to the basket, but he also has a good outside shot. His coaches want him to utilize it more rather than incurring all of the physical pounding that his drives inflict. "When a coach is behind you and gives you the green light, you can't worry about any criticism anytime you miss," he said.

Johnson, who shared the backcourt with Jeff Hornacek, another perennial All-Star, doesn't dote on perceived shortcomings. He has proven his worth. In 1989, for instance, his first full season in Phoenix, he led the team in foul shooting percentage (.882), assists (901) and steals (135). In 1991 he led the Suns in scoring (22.1), assists (781) and steals (163) while being named as a starter in the NBA All-Star Game.

LARRY JOHNSON

Position: Forward   **Birth Date:** March 14, 1969
College: UNLV   **Height:** 6′ 6″
Drafted: Charlotte, 1st Rd. ('91)   **Weight:** 250

Larry Johnson, with that distinctive front gold tooth, is television's "jammen-est" Grandmama ever. And despite a delightful TV shoe ad that gave thunkin' and dunkin' a new "grey-haired" dimension, he is the one Grandmama no NBA team wants to see very often.

Johnson, the star of UNLV's 1990 national championship team and a two-time first team All-America, was the first player picked in the 1991 NBA draft. He signed a six-year contract for nearly $20 million, though some NBA people said he was too small at 6′ 6″ to play power forward in the NBA.

Tell it to the teams who faced him, beginning with the New Jersey Nets who, after Johnson had been a member of the Hornets for just three days, watched him pull down 18 rebounds against them.

And after his rookie season, ask the rest of the NBA, who saw him average 19.1 points and 11 rebounds per game (his 899 rebounds were 11th in the NBA), block 51 shots and turn in 46 "double-double" performances (double figures in scoring and rebounds).

He is incredibly strong for his size, and one NFL scout declared he would make it in pro football. If his size is a detriment, he compensates with long arms that help him play as "big" as power forwards who are four and five inches taller. Before his rookie season had ended, he was being compared with such all-stars as Charles Barkley and Karl Malone for his great determination to grab rebounds.

Boston's Larry Bird, after just two head-to-head confrontations, noted: "He's strong, quick and very aggressive. He is powerful and when he goes after the ball, he can jump over anybody."

"He's our building block, our foundation, our untouchable," says the Hornets' Vice President Allan Bristow. "And I'm not the only one who thinks that way."

Even Grandmama would agree.

Below left: *Larry Johnson averaged nearly 20 points per game and led Charlotte in rebounding as a rookie.*

Below: *Johnson, the NBA's No. 1 draft pick in 1991, was chosen its Rookie of the Year in 1992.*

Left: *Larry Johnson wears jersey No. 2 in honor of Jerry Tarkanian, his coach at UNLV where both of them enjoyed the 1990 NCAA championship.*

Below left: *Johnson also laid waste to predictions that, at 6' 6", he couldn't play forward in the NBA: He pulled down 899 rebounds and scored 1,576 points as a rookie in 1992.*

Below: *Johnson broke every Charlotte rookie record and won two games for the Hornets with last-second shots.*

Opposite: *With his great strength and drive, Johnson made himself a problem for NBA defenders in his rookie season.*

48

MICHAEL JORDAN

Left: Michael Jordan is the master of levitation in the NBA, with an endless repertoire of shots that seem to take him eye level with the basket.

Below: Jordan is the nation's most recognizable athlete, both from his playing and from his steady stream of endorsements.

Opposite: Michael Jordan played on NCAA, Olympic and NBA title teams. Before he won NBA titles in 1991 and 1992, his game-winning basket in the final seconds helped North Carolina win the NCAA title in his freshman year; and two years after that, he was on America's gold medal winners in the 1984 Olympics.

Position: Guard   **Birth Date:** Feb. 17, 1963
College: North Carolina   **Height:** 6′ 6″
Drafted: Chicago, 1st Rd. ('84)   **Weight:** 198

There is no more visible athlete in the world than Michael Jordan. Never mind the NBA – the entire world knows who he is and what he does, and marvels at the way he does it. His many product endorsements have increased his recognition, and his swooping, driving, leaping, soaring style of play has made him the game's most astounding player ever.

Michael Jordan rewrites the record book every year. He and Wilt Chamberlain are the only players ever to score 3,000 points in one season; and only he and Wilt ever led the NBA in scoring for at least six seasons – and Michael should break Chamberlain's record of seven by the time he retires.

His offensive style is unique, and his personal trademark is his protruding tongue that shows nearly every

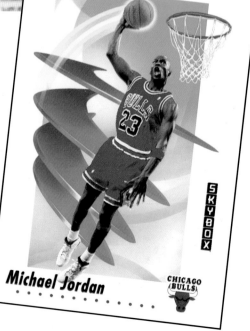

Michael Jordan — CHICAGO BULLS — SKYBOX

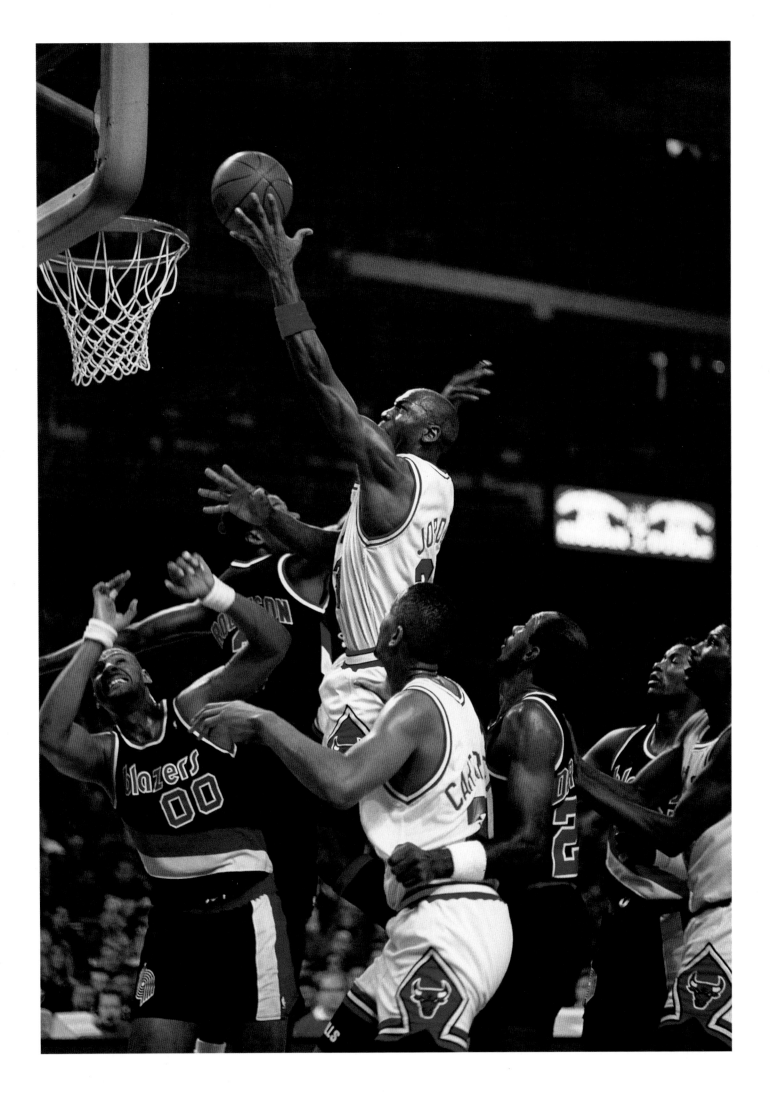

time he swoops to the basket. A spontaneous player, Jordan once said: "I don't plan all that stuff. It just happens." But it happens because of his marvelous athletic ability that often allows him to make a shot when hanging in the air, or changing direction with both feet off the ground.

While his offensive numbers are dynamic, he gets more personal satisfaction from his work on defense, underscored by his perennial standing on the NBA's All-Defensive team. His speed and ability to anticipate have helped him become the first player ever to record 200 steals in one season. "He is like hell turned loose on defense," says John Bach, the Bulls' defensive coach. "When we want to shut down the opposition's big scorer in the final two minutes of a game, we let Michael do it – and that is regardless of the position or the size of the other guy."

Jordan is the team's absolute leader and insists that his teammates work as hard as he does – even in practice. For several years, he battled the front office to get better players and relieve some of the burdens which he believed were preventing the team from winning a title. When the team finally responded by acquiring such stars as Scottie Pippen and Horace Grant, and adding some good role players, they won NBA titles in 1991 and 1992.

But they need Michael Jordan most of all.

Opposite top: *Michael Jordan is an indefatigable player. He played more than 3,000 minutes in seven of his first eight seasons.*

Opposite bottom: *Jordan has recorded more game-winning shots than any Chicago Bulls player in history.*

Right: *Michael Jordan was a two-time All-America at North Carolina. He has been the NBA's Most Valuable Player several times; winner of many scoring titles; and a perennial member of the All-Star team. There is little doubt that he is the greatest player at his position in the history of the game.*

53

SHAWN KEMP

Position: Forward　　　　**Birth Date:** Nov. 26, 1969
College: None　　　　　　**Height:** 6' 10"
Drafted: Seattle, 1st Rd. ('89)　　**Weight:** 245

Shawn Kemp is a rarity in NBA history. He is only the fifth player ever to be drafted without playing college basketball. He had been a star at Elkhart High School in Indiana, and was awarded a scholarship to the University of Kentucky. Off-the-court problems prevented him from playing at UK, and he transferred to Trinity Junior College in Texas before declaring himself eligible for the 1989 NBA draft. But lack of college experience has not proven to be a detriment.

"The things he always had going for him along with his natural skills to rebound and block shots, were his love for the game and his work ethic," says his former coach, K.C. Jones. "You can't teach those things. He didn't have any college experience as a base so he worked on the fundamental parts of the game – when to shoot, when to drive, learning to take what's there."

Patience also was his biggest virtue. He started just one of his 81 games as a rookie. He became the starting power forward in the 16th game of his second season, and led his team in scoring 13 times, in rebounding 35 times, and was the NBA's 18th best shot-blocker that year.

"When I was first drafted, I wanted everything because I couldn't see anything," Kemp said. "Then I got a feel for what this game is all about – the people who can help you, the people who can hurt you, how to prepare every night for a game. That became my job and my life."

REGGIE LEWIS

Position: Guard
College: Northeastern
Drafted: Boston, 1st Rd. ('87)

Birth Date: Nov. 21, 1965
Height: 6′ 7″
Weight: 195

Boston Celtics boss Red Auerbach always made it a policy to draft at least one college player from the Boston area in the years when the NBA draft lasted 12 rounds. Rick Weitzman from Northeastern University was one of those players in 1967, and as team scout two decades later he convinced the Celtics to select fellow alumnus Reggie Lewis in the first round of the 1987 draft. They got themselves a bona fide star in the Celtics' tradition of finding talent few others had noticed. Lewis had amassed great scoring numbers but received little notoriety because his school had minimum visibility. He was passed over by 26 teams in the 1987 NBA draft, because their scouts were wary of his playing background; and an injury in a pre-draft camp all but scratched his name from their lists. But their loss

Above: *The Celtics' newest star, Reggie Lewis, is a home-grown product – having played at Northeastern University in Boston. He succeeded Larry Bird as the team's primary offensive threat during the 1992 season, when he spearheaded the team's drive to the Eastern Division title.*

Left: *Lewis began his Celtics career as small forward, where he had starred in college while leading Northeastern to several NCAA playoff appearances. He adjusted perfectly to the role of shooting guard with the Celtics, and started to lead the team in scoring in 1991.*

quickly became the Celtics' gain.

"Lewis is unstoppable," New Jersey Nets coach Chuck Daly said of the all-pro guard, who began his NBA career as a small forward.

He has become more than just a scorer, though this has always been the easiest part of his game. He led the team in scoring for the second straight year in 1992, as well as in steals and blocked shots.

"I never really doubted my ability to play in the NBA," noted Lewis, who is very quiet and unassuming. "When I was a freshman at Northeastern, I played against some of the pros in the Celtics' rookie camp and I held my own. I really felt I'd have a chance."

He is the Celtics' number two, or shooting guard, but his passing skills are vastly underrated. He works constantly to upgrade his ballhandling and three-point shooting to round out a great offensive arsenal that includes a deadly shot from the corner.

"He is the newest recipient of that quiet, solid leadership that has been passed from one generation of Celtics to the next," notes team executive Dave Gavitt.

The local boy obviously has made good.

Opposite: *Lewis has great quickness which helps him to get free of defenders. He uses it either to drive cleanly to the basket, or freeze a defender so that he can stop and shoot his accurate jump shot. Reggie also has a deadly shot from the corner.*

Right: *Unlike Larry Bird and Kevin McHale, the Celtics' two great offensive stars of the eighties, Lewis is very quiet and does not talk much trash when he is on the court. But when the Celtics made their run for the 1992 Eastern Division title, he averaged more than 24 points in the team's final eight games.*

DAN MAJERLE

Position: Guard/Forward   **Birth Date:** Sept. 9, 1965
College: Central Michigan   **Height:** 6' 6"
Drafted: Phoenix, 1st Rd. ('88)   **Weight:** 220

The image will always last of Dan Majerle battling and scrapping for the United States basketball team in the 1988 Olympic Games – the brightest light in an otherwise disappointing bronze medal finish.

Majerle (pronounced MAR-LEE) had come from Central Michigan University, and had won a spot on the team against players from more glamorous basketball backgrounds. The Phoenix Suns admired his "blue collar" skills so much they drafted him even before he made the Olympic team.

The toughness Majerle exhibited during the Olympics has helped him throughout his NBA career, as he has battled against illness and injury that caused him to miss several games in his first three seasons. In Phoenix, Majerle has developed a valuable "sixth man" role, and because of his tough-nosed defensive ability he usually plays against the opposition's top scorer.

Above: *Dan Majerle gained much notoriety for his tough defense for the U.S. during the 1988 Olympic games, in which his team won a bronze medal. Majerle's hard-nosed defense carried over to the NBA, where he usually gets the opposition's best scorer. But playing against opposing guards such as the Lakers' Magic Johnson also helped him to develop a stronger offense.*

Left: *Majerle was a first-round pick of the Phoenix Suns in 1988, after starring at Central Michigan University.*

JEFF MALONE

Right: Jeff Malone played the first seven years of his NBA career with the Washington Bullets and still is among their all-time leaders in points, games and minutes played. He scored the 10,000th point of his NBA career with Utah in 1990.

Position: Guard
College: Mississippi State
Drafted: Washington, 1st Rd. ('83)

Birth Date: June 28, 1961
Height: 6′ 4″
Weight: 205

Jeff Malone spent the first seven seasons of his career with the Washington Bullets, who had picked him on the first round out of Mississippi State, where he was an All-America in 1983 and was the number three collegiate scorer.

In Washington he was the star, a two-time All-Star performer who doubled his scoring average in his seasons with the Bullets. He came to Utah before the 1991 season as part of a three-way deal between the Bullets,

Sacramento Kings and Utah.

"Washington was great for me," Malone said. "but to come to the Jazz, with all the fans every night, I love it. It's a whole different feeling."

In Utah Malone has been able to make more all-around contributions than before, including some very underrated defense, while also helping to lighten John Stockton's play-making load.

"You look around and you see that people in the league get known for something," notes Frank Layden, the club president who engineered the trade. "Everyone thought he was a good scorer and a great shooter, but he's also a good passer and great defensively."

KARL MALONE

Left: *The Mailman – Karl Malone. He delivers.*

Below: *Malone was picked for the 1992 U.S. Olympic team.*

Opposite: *Malone is renowned for his aggressive play close to the basket, as he shows against the Chicago Bulls' Horace Grant (with goggles).*

Position: Forward
College: Louisiana Tech
Drafted: Utah, 1st Rd. ('85)

Birth Date: July 24, 1963
Height: 6′ 9″
Weight: 256

"The Mailman – because he delivers." A sportswriter in Louisiana hung that moniker on Karl Malone when he played for Louisiana Tech in the early eighties, and it belongs to him forever.

A marvelously sculpted power forward for the Utah Jazz, Malone has toiled long and hard during off-seasons on the weight equipment in the basement of his Salt Lake City home. He has been crowned Mr. All-Pro several times during his career, and has been a frequent participant in the NBA's All-Star Game, where he was picked as MVP in 1989.

Malone has worked hard to raise the level of his game to the point where he has no peers as a power foward. "In this business, everyone always says what you can't do," Malone said. "Guys say you can't shoot outside so you start shooting from the outside and making them. Then it's that you can't play defense so you start playing defense. You throw it back at those same critics."

Case in point: As a rookie, Malone's foul shooting accuracy was a miserable 49 percent. He now shoots consistently in the high 70s.

"He is 100 percent better than when he started," says Jazz coach Jerry Sloan. "You know some guys go out the same way they come in. Not Karl. He has always

Opposite: *Karl Malone, who played at Louisiana Tech, is one of the NBA's best power forwards. He is always among the league's top producers in games played, points, and rebounds. Karl has been selected several times to the NBA All-Star Game and was named Most Valuable Player in the 1989 game.*

Right: *Malone skies over the Lakers' A.C. Green and stuffs home one of his patented jams. He is a very durable player – several times playing every game of the regular season – and brushes aside opponents' complaints that he is too rough around the basket.*

done the things he needed to become better and now he's become one of the NBA's best post-up players."

Utah president Frank Layden, who was Malone's first coach with the Jazz, has two images of Malone. Around the basket, he says, Karl reminds him of a heavyweight boxing champion by the way he utilizes his strength and moves. Layden also compares him to Jim Brown, the great NFL Hall of Fame running back. "Karl has the same kind of physical strength, quickness, good hands and mental toughness," Layden says. "The big thing about Karl is that he can catch the ball. He'll catch anything that's thrown to him, and then he lets his other skills take over."

Malone has averaged nearly 30 points a game during the late eighties and early nineties, second only to Chicago's Michael Jordan.

One of his chief assets is playing with all-pro guard John Stockton. Ironically, Malone and Stockton knew each other even before they became teammates at Utah because both were cut by coach Bobby Knight from the 1984 U.S. Olympic gold medal team. In 1992, both were unanimous choices for America's Olympic basketball team.

The two have established such a rapport together that they often are referred to as "Stockalone." Malone utilizes Stockton's ability to get him the ball on the fast break; and Stockton thrives on Malone's knack of catching a pass in traffic and finishing a play.

"I'm very happy to play with him all these years," Stockton says. "He's made my job easier."

DANNY MANNING

Left: *Manning, a No. 1 draft pick of the Los Angeles Clippers in 1988, fought his way back from reconstructive knee surgery and helped his team to its first playoff spot ever in 1992 when he led it in scoring. He also was a member of the Kansas Jayhawks' 1988 NCAA champions.*

Position: Forward   **Birth Date:** May 17, 1966
College: Kansas   **Height:** 6' 10"
Drafted: L.A. Clippers, 1st Rd. ('88)   **Weight:** 230

Danny Manning once was the toast of college basketball – and he believes those good old days are back again. He may be correct because in 1992 his team, the Los Angeles Clippers, made the playoffs for the first time ever and he seemed to rediscover the talent flow that had eluded him during his first three NBA seasons.

Manning had helped lead the University of Kansas to the 1988 NCAA title, capping a senior season in which he had 11 30-plus scoring games, and 15 double-doubles (double figures in scoring and rebounds). He won every major individual award, was the first player chosen in the 1988 draft, and became the star of the U.S. Olympic team.

But in the 26th game of his NBA rookie season, after scoring in double figures in all but three games, he crashed to the floor after scoring a layup late in the first quarter of a game against Milwaukee. He tore the anterior cruciate ligaments in his right knee so badly that he had to have reconstructive surgery, costing him the rest of his rookie season and the first 12 games of his second season.

Since then, his knee has been sound, but the rehabilitation process has been slow – and so have the achievements so many had predicted, as the Clippers plodded along in mediocrity. When his old college coach, Larry Brown, became LA's head coach midway through the 1992 season, Manning seemed to get new life by leading the team in scoring for the first time.

Manning's father, Ed, played professionally, then coached college basketball. "That exposure rubbed off on the way [Danny] approaches the game. He is the ideal player for a coach," his former L.A. coach, Mike Shuler, noted. "The most important thing to him is winning, and he feels so strongly about that."

REGGIE MILLER

Position: Guard	**Birth Date:** Aug. 24, 1965
College: UCLA	**Height:** 6' 7"
Drafted: Indiana, 1st Rd. ('87)	**Weight:** 185

Reggie Miller comes from a family in which athletic excellence is the norm. His sister, Cheryl, is one of the finest women basketball players of all time; and his brother, Darrell, was a catcher for five years with the California Angels, and now is an executive with that team.

And then there is Reggie.

The youngest of Saul and Carrie Miller's four children, it hardly seemed possible that he would ever match his siblings' athletic achievements. For the first four years of his life, he slept with steel braces on his legs after having been born with pronated hips. Doctors said he might never walk normally.

But Reggie had to compete to survive in his family, and though overmatched for many years in the furious basketball games played in the Miller driveway, he developed his own game. He became a strong, talented player who was an All-America at UCLA and finished

Above: *Reggie Miller is one of the NBA's best three-point shooter and holds the Pacers' all-time record. In the 1990 season, he made 150 three-pointers and once had a streak in which he hit one or more of those shots in 108 straight games.*

Right: *In addition to Miller's exploits at UCLA and in the NBA, his sister Cheryl was an All-America player at Southern Cal and a gold medal Olympian; and his brother, Darrell, was a major league catcher.*

second on the school's all-time scoring list behind Lew Alcindor (Kareem Abdul-Jabbar).

Now one of the best shooting guards in the NBA, everything he has done always seems to come back to his family experiences. For example, Reggie set an Indiana Pacers' team record with 150 three-pointers in the 1990 season, and has always been among the NBA's top free-throw shooters.

"How do you think he got that high arc on his shot?" his brother Darrell once asked. "He had to learn to shoot that way or we'd block it."

His great enthusiasm for the game at UCLA attracted the attention of Magic Johnson and Michael Cooper of the Lakers, who played against him in pickup games. "They took me under their wing and told me to just watch and listen," Miller said. "I did, and I learned a lot."

Reggie Miller still has the same love for fierce competition that he developed in those family scrimmages, and it certainly shows. "In the NBA you have to take fun seriously, and Reggie does that," notes Bob Hill, his coach with the Indiana Pacers. "He loves the game so much, he loves the shooting drills. He loves to scrimmage. He loves to play."

CHRIS MULLIN

Position: Forward   **Birth Date:** July 30, 1963
College: St. John's (N.Y.)   **Height:** 6' 7"
Drafted: Golden State, 1st Rd. ('85)   **Weight:** 215

Chris Mullin is a living reminder of the game's work ethic. A two-time All-America at St. John's University, Mullin improved his game during his first two NBA seasons, but his personal life was a struggle. During his third year, he entered an alcoholic rehabilitation program. From that came a newer, stronger and better Chris Mullin – one who has been among the NBA's best forwards ever since. In fact, one observer termed him "a smaller version of Larry Bird."

Magic Johnson put him on his "respect list" comprised of players whom he hated to play against. "When God made basketball and said, 'This is a player,' he was thinking about Chris," Magic said. "He's just a great basketball player."

As a result of his rehabilitation work, Mullin's

Opposite: *Reggie Miller finished second to Kareem Abdul-Jabbar as UCLA's career scorer. In 1990 Miller became the first Indiana Pacers player in 13 years to be named to the NBA All-Star team.*

Above: *After leading the Warriors in scoring for five consecutive seasons, Chris Mullin was one of the NBA stars named to the 1992 Olympic team for the Barcelona Games.*

Right: *Named 1985 College Player of the Year after an All-America season at St. John's University in New York City, Mullin was the seventh player chosen in that year's draft.*

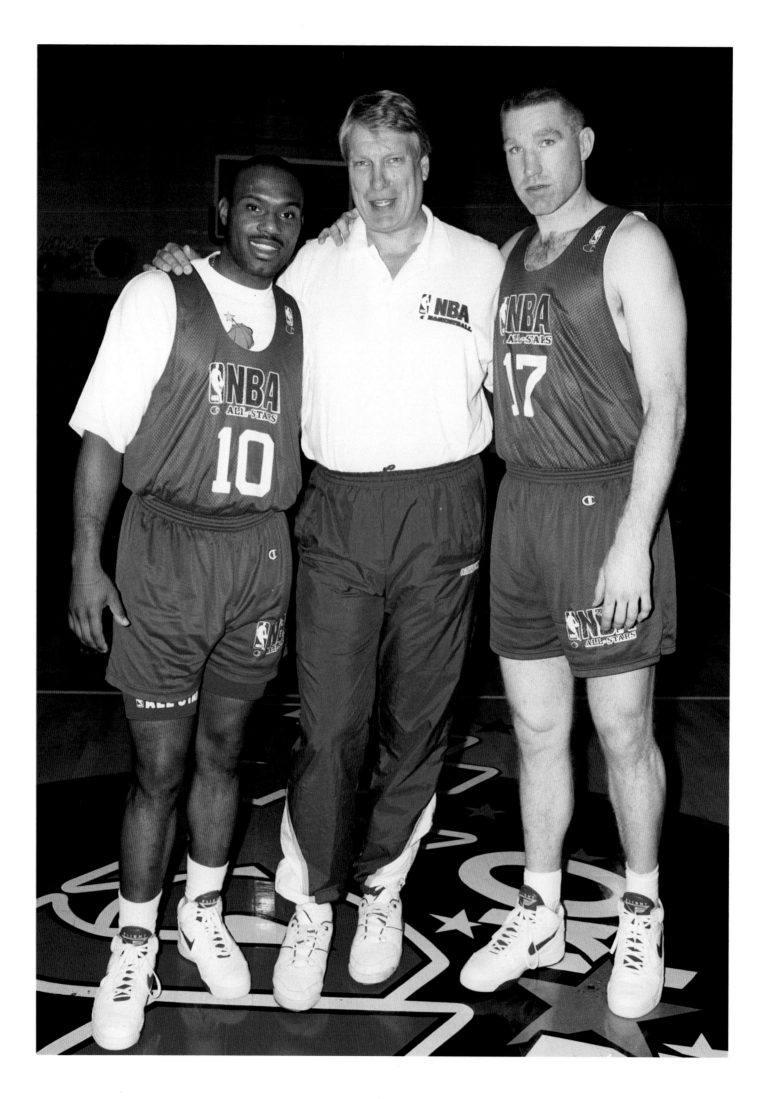

game became more versatile, and his stamina improved to the point where he averages more than 40 minutes per game. For his first two NBA seasons, opponents knew that he lacked confidence to drive to the basket, so they had only to defense his jump shot. That all changed when he gained the confidence to add strong moves to the basket to go with his jumper. His scoring average increased more than five points per game in 1988 and was up more than 11 points the following year. By 1992 he had led the Warriors in scoring for five straight seasons.

He is now recognized as one of the league's most versatile offensive performers. Dennis Rodman of Detroit, one of the NBA's top defenders, notes: "You can't describe him. He scores 30 points a night and you wonder how. I know I'm playing him good defense and he's still scoring. People don't want to give him credit because he doesn't have great speed, but he has enough ability to get himself open."

And to get himself named to the 1992 U.S. gold-medal Olympic team.

Opposite: *Golden State coach Don Nelson between his two stars, Tim Hardaway (left) and Chris Mullin. During the 1991 season, Mullin became the first Warriors player to start an NBA All-Star Game since Rick Barry in 1978.*

Above: *Mullin is an outstanding free throw shooter, and sank 50 in a row during the 1990 season. He has better than an 85 percent accuracy mark in his NBA career.*

Left: *Mullin once scored 10 or more points in 175 straight games.*

Page 70: *Mullin has hit more than 50 percent of his shots in the NBA. In a game against Miami in 1991, he set a franchise record by going 11-for-11 in field goal tries.*

DIKEMBE MUTOMBO

DIKEMBE MUTOMBO   CENTER

Position: Center   **Birth Date:** June 25, 1966
College: Georgetown   **Height:** 7' 2"
Drafted: Denver, 1st Rd. ('91)   **Weight:** 245

No one really had a good handle on Dikembe Mutombo's basketball skills when he was picked in the first round of the 1991 draft by the Denver Nuggets. The Nuggets' gamble paid off as Dikembe vied with Charlotte's Larry Johnson for top rookie honors throughout their first NBA season.

He had come to Georgetown University from Zaire, where he had played that country's version of high school basketball. He was redshirted for his freshman year while he learned English, and upgraded his basketball skills to match some awesome physical talents.

At Georgetown Mutombo specialized in rebounds and blocked shots. In his senior season, he was named Big East Defensive Player of the Year; ranked fourth nationally with 151 blocked shots; and sixth in rebounding with a 12.2 per game average.

His offense was ordinary; in his best season, as a junior, he averaged just 15.2 points per game.

During his summers, he worked at Georgetown with alumnus Patrick Ewing, a star with the Knicks. "We worked on some moves, like his hook and turn-around," Ewing said. "I was just trying to let him know what to expect when he reached the NBA level."

Denver felt Mutombo's physical skills, particularly his defense, was worth the first-round gamble, and they were correct. Mutombo was second among the Nuggets' scorers as a rookie with a 16.6 average; led the team in rebounds; and was sixth in the NBA in blocked shots with 210.

Above: *The 7' 2" center takes a breather. Mutombo played the equivalent of high school basketball in his native Zaire.*

Left: *Mutombo is a defensive force around the basket, and blocked 210 shots in his rookie NBA season.*

Opposite: *Although Mutombo was the Nuggets' No. 2 scorer in his rookie 1992 season, he also brought great rebounding skills into the NBA. He ranks fourth in Georgetown history; set a Big East tournament single game record of 27 in 1991; and then led the Nuggets in his rookie year with a 12.3 per game average.*

HAKEEM OLAJUWON

Position: Center   **Birth Date:** Jan. 21, 1963
College: University of Houston   **Height:** 7' 0"
Drafted: Houston, 1st Rd. ('84)   **Weight:** 250

Translate Hakeem Olajuwon's name into English and it means: "Always being on top." How appropriate.

How appropriate too, that the Houston Rockets came out "on top" in a coin flip with the Portland Trail Blazers when their "heads" call brought the number one pick in the 1984 draft.

They picked the seven-foot Olajuwon, who had led the University of Houston team to three consecutive NCAA Final Four appearances. That was remarkable in itself because Olajuwon, a native of Lagos, Nigeria, had never even played basketball until he was 17 years old. He began playing then only because, as a member of his school's handball team, he was "borrowed" by the basketball team to play in an All-Nigerian Teachers Sports Festival.

Above: *Hakeem Olajuwon is a perennial All-NBA selection and was named Southwest Conference Player of the Eighties.*

Right: *He finished second to the Bulls' Michael Jordan in Rookie of the Year balloting in 1985.*

Opposite: *Olajuwon has averaged more than 11 rebounds per game throughout his NBA career, and usually makes the NBA's All-Defensive team each season. He also leads his team in blocked shots, and led the NBA with 376 during the 1990 season.*

Opposite: *Olajuwon was the third NBA player ever to record 10,000 points, 5,000 rebounds and 1,000 steals, leading his team in steals six straight years.*

Above: *Olajuwon is remarkably quick for such a big man.*

Above right: *Houston's star veteran – Olajuwon.*

He came to the United States and was an immediate collegiate star – and a charter member of Houston's famed "Phi Slama Jama" team. Olajuwon later was selected as Player of the Eighties in the Southwest Conference after leading his team to an 88-16 record in three seasons.

He averaged 20.6 points per game in his rookie NBA season and was runner-up to Michael Jordan for Rookie of the Year. Since then, his statistics have been awesome:

● He has averaged more than 20 points per game, and led the Rockets in scoring each season.

● He led the team in blocked shots in each of his first eight years, and led the NBA in 1990 and 1991.

● He is remarkably quick for such a big man, proven by leading the team in steals seven of his first eight seasons.

● He was starting center for the Western Conference All-Star team four years in a row.

● In 1990 he became only the second player ever to accumulate more than 1,000 rebounds and 300 blocked shots in a single season.

● In 1989 he was the first ever to get 200 steals and 200 blocked shots in the same year.

● In 1988 he finished with double figures in all but one game.

● In 1987 he was only the second player ever to lead his team in four major categories – scoring, rebounds, blocked shots and steals.

● He is the third player in NBA history to record 10,000 points, 5,000 rebounds and 1,000 steals, assists and blocked shots. The others are Kareem Abdul-Jabbar and Julius Erving.

Olajuwon is a great force on the court. "He is one of those few players who can dictate the way an opponent plays," notes Celtics coach Chris Ford. "You have to find a different way to attack the middle around the basket, and even away from the basket because he is so quick to get out on shooters who think they're safe popping six and seven-footers.

"Hakeem is big enough to battle other centers head-up and on offense, he can overpower a big man who cannot match his quickness and leaping ability."

CHUCK PERSON

Position: Forward   **Birth Date:** June 27, 1964
College: Auburn   **Height:** 6′ 8″
Drafted: Indiana, 1st Rd. ('86)   **Weight:** 225

He is known by his character: predictably unpredictable, cocky and brash. And he is known by his achievements: all-time leading scorer at Auburn University, where he played with Charles Barkley; NBA Rookie of the Year in 1987; and the Indiana Pacers' scoring leader in each of his first three seasons. Presenting Chuck Person.

One of the NBA's premier trash-talkers, Person always saves his best performances for when he plays against the Boston Celtics. In the 1991 playoffs, he ver-

bally trashed the NBA's greatest icon, Larry Bird. Bird then proceeded to torch him on the court as the Celtics eliminated Indiana – and then invited Chuck to play in his annual All-Star game a few weeks later in Indianapolis.

In a game against Chicago, Person flattened the Bulls' John Paxson as he shot a three-pointer, and was ejected from the game and fined $7,500 by the NBA for what was considered a flagrant foul.

Was he repentant? Not in the least.

"I don't apologize to any team or to any one individual for what I do on the basketball court," he says.

Whether he is lighting up the basket or tempers, Person is a force to be reckoned with.

SCOTTIE PIPPEN

Position: Forward **Birth Date:** Sept. 25, 1965
College: Central Arkansas **Height:** 6' 7"
Drafted: Seattle, 1st Rd. ('87) **Weight:** 210

Following the 1987 draft, the Chicago Bulls traded their No. 1 pick, Olden Polynice, to Seattle for its first pick, Scottie Pippen, who had starred at the University of Central Arkansas. The move was intended to add depth to a team centered around Michael Jordan.

As a high school senior, Pippen was 6' 1½" and wasn't given much encouragement when he was accepted at Central Arkansas. By the time he arrived, he had grown two inches. He then added 20 pounds and grew another 3½" to stand at 6' 7" by the end of his senior season.

"He took the skills he had learned as a small player and used them when he was bigger," one of his college coaches noted. 'His arms are so long and his hands so

Above: *Scottie Pippen may play within the shadow of Michael Jordan with the Chicago Bulls, but he still is one of the NBA's top forwards and many believe he will reach Jordan's plateau before his career ends.*

Left: *Pippen's talents are so prolific that he has created a new position in the NBA – "point forward" – the benchmark for the modern all-purpose basketball player. He also has been picked to the NBA's All-Defensive team while averaging more than 20 points per game.*

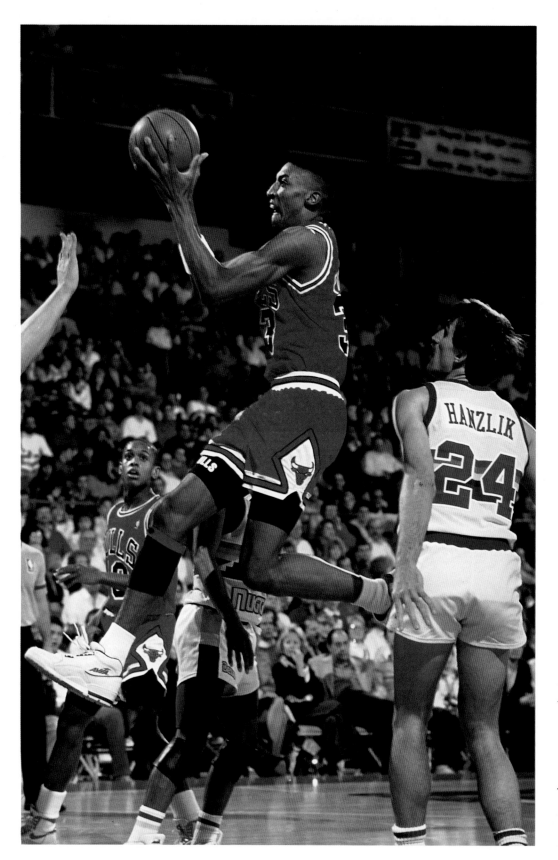

Left: *Pippen was a first-round draft pick by the Seattle Supersonics in 1987 and was immediately traded to Chicago after Jordan demanded the team surround him with better players. He has since begun to match or exceed Michael's per game averages in rebounds, assists and blocked shots.*

Opposite: *Pippen began making regular appearances in the NBA All-Star Game in 1990, and joined Jordan on the 1992 U.S. Olympic basketball team for the Barcelona Games. He has become, as one NBA observer noted "a second whirling dervish for opposing teams to consider. Jordan on one side of the court, Pippen on the other, interchangeable, lethal. . . ."*

big that he really plays like someone who is 6' 10" or 6' 11"."

With that package, the Bulls had one of the key players who eventually brought them two NBA championships, and a player who has become a star in his own right. Opponents soon found they could not expend all of their defensive energy trying to stop Jordan because Pippen was capable of producing big scoring games.

"His role has grown and grown," Bulls coach Phil Jackson says. "Right from the start, he could rebound

yet still dribble the length of the court. He could post up and he had those slashing sorts of moves. You knew he could become a very good player, but you didn't know how good. He played a few times at guard in his first couple of seasons, bringing the ball up against teams with pressing guards. But mostly we used him at small forward.

"As more and more teams pressed, we wound up with Michael bringing up the ball and we didn't want to do that. So Scottie became a third ball advancer as part of an offense that attacked at multiple points. From

that position, he started being able to take control, to make decisions. He became a bit of everything.''

Soon thereafter, Pippen was in a scoring slump and Jackson told him to forget about points but concentrate on making things happen. That night, he scored 13 points, but also had 13 rebounds and 12 assists. "That's what he can do," Jackson said. "From that point, we won seven games in a row, and got us rolling for the rest of the year.''

Pippen is tall enough and jumps high enough to move inside. He handles the ball well enough to be the Bulls' third guard but also is a point forward, a position that he created for himself. Guard him high, and he takes the defender low; guard him low, and he can go high and shoot. Leave him alone for a moment and he is gone, soaring for a stuff shot that is more reminiscent of the moves Julius (Dr. J.) Irving used to make than those patented by Michael Jordan.

Best of all, Scottie Pippen has established his own identity playing with Jordan, and has been named to the NBA's All-Defensive Team and the All-Star team. Just like Michael.

MARK PRICE

Left: *Scottie Pippen – All-Star. Pippen's toughness was questioned early in his NBA career when migraine headaches forced him out of games. But the problem was cleared up after he began wearing wire-rimmed glasses off the court, and he is now one of the league's most durable players.*

Right: *Mark Price of the Cleveland Cavaliers not only is one of the NBA's top point guards, but an artist in running the team's pick-and-roll plays. He also uses his quickness and skill driving to the basket. "No one runs the pick-and-roll better," notes Dave Gavitt of the Celtics. "Price will come off a screen at any time, and after he catches the ball, his teammate will turn and set up for an immediate pick-and-roll. No one else does that."*

Position: Guard
College: Georgia Tech
Drafted: Dallas, 2nd Rd. ('86)

Birth Date: Feb. 16, 1964
Height: 6' 1"
Weight: 170

The pick-and-roll play is one of the oldest in the NBA playbook and guard Mark Price of the Cleveland Cavaliers is its master.

That is but one of Price's assets. He runs the Cavs' offense as a point guard, a position he had to learn once he got into the NBA because he had been a "shooting" guard at Georgia Tech. In fact, the Dallas Mavericks had second thoughts about this ability after picking him

on the second round of the 1986 draft, and immediately traded him to Cleveland.

"I realized that there were many other people on the team who could score, and I didn't have to worry about scoring," Price said. "My job is to run the team and get everybody involved. I look for my shot in situations where things might not be going well and we need a boost."

He is consistently among the NBA's assists leaders. After winning his biggest battle – recovering from knee surgery early in the 1991 season – he came right back to lead the league in free throw accuracy in 1992.

83

MITCH RICHMOND

Position: Guard   **Birth Date:** June 30, 1965
College: Kansas State   **Height:** 6' 5"
Drafted: Golden State, 1st Rd. ('88)   **Weight:** 215

Mitch Richmond is a worker – and an achiever. That is why, early in the 1992 season, the Sacramento Kings parted with No. 1 pick Billy Owens, the third player picked in the draft, to get him from the Golden State Warriors.

"When you have a player like Rich," said Kings guard Spud Webb, "it makes you a much better team."

Richmond has proven he can do it. He raised himself from a mediocre player in junior college, to All-America at Kansas State, to U.S. Olympian, to 1989 NBA Rookie of the Year.

Mitch was the only unanimous selection to the all-rookie team that year after averaging 22 points per game, and then became the first Rookie of the Year since 1979 to improve his scoring average during his second and third seasons.

But working to improve is the story of his basketball life, and being traded from a playoff team to one that is struggling to reach that plateau was just another challenge for Richmond. "I enjoy the stress and pressure of playing," he commented, "and of having my teammates rely on me."

Left: *Mitch Richmond won NBA Rookie of the Year honors in 1989, and then became the first winner since Phil Ford, in 1979, to improve his scoring average in each of the next two seasons. He also ranked among the NBA's top 20 scorers in each of his first four seasons. "I think we're very similar in styles," Michael Jordan of the Chicago Bulls once noted of Richmond. "His physical ability causes trouble both offensively and defensively. It's tough for me to spin away from him, and tough to get low and post up. I have a lot of respect for him. He's competition."*

DAVID ROBINSON

Left: *David Robinson is a superb athlete, and while he has been among the NBA leaders in rebounds and blocked shots, he also recorded more than 125 steals in each of his first three seasons.*

Below: *Robinson was the first player selected in the 1987 draft, and in 1992 he was named to his second U.S. Olympic team. He was NBA Rookie of the Year in 1990, and played in the NBA All-Star Game in each of his first three seasons.*

Position: Center **Birth Date:** Aug. 6, 1965
College: U.S. Naval Academy **Height:** 7′ 1″
Drafted: San Antonio, 1st Rd. ('87) **Weight:** 235

David Robinson – "The Admiral" – has set his course to become the NBA's Center of the Nineties, and many in the league believe he will do it.

Robinson didn't start playing basketball until his senior year in high school, and as a freshman at the United States Naval Academy (to which he gained admission on the strength of a 1320 score on his college boards) he averaged just seven points a game. But by his senior year, he had grown seven inches and was the third highest scorer in the nation (28.3 points per game) and fourth highest rebounder (11.8). He was a un-animous All-America selection and named NCAA Player of the Year.

David was the NBA's first pick in 1987 by the San Antonio Spurs, though he still had to serve two years of active Navy duty (he had outgrown the Navy's height

maximum and was exempt from the five-year minimum service requirement for USNA graduates). "The anticipation and the expectations of him were unbelievable," said his first NBA coach, Larry Brown. "He came into the league with less playing time than most first-round choices."

Still, he was named the NBA's Rookie of the Year in 1990; was the only rookie in the All-Star Game; and turned in some eye-popping statistics (tops in rebounding; second in blocked shots; ninth in scoring, with double figures in 81 of 82 games, 20 points or more 62 times, and 30 or more 15 times).

His second season – a year when many young players level off, or even slump a bit as they battle the adjustments teams have made to their game – was just as spectacular. He was the only player that year to make the top ten in four different statistical categories, and was the Western Conference's starting center in the All-Star Game.

His third season was cut short by surgery on his right hand. Still working on the mental aspects of the game, Robinson said, "I am more able to focus on the opponent and to be prepared every night." Teammate Terry Cummings and Orlando coach Matt Goukas both agree that he intimidates teams with his play around the basket.

"He is the greatest impact player the league has seen since Kareem Abdul-Jabbar," said former Phoenix coach Cotton Fitzsimmons, adding that within his first two seasons, Robinson passed such stars as Michael Jordan, Magic Johnson, and Larry Bird as the game's most imposing player. "They're all MVPs," he said, "but this guy is more."

Opposite top: *David Robinson, nicknamed "The Admiral," is the first player from Navy ever to play in the NBA. He was consensus NCAA Player of the Year in 1987, then served two years of active duty as a naval officer.*

Opposite below: *In the 1991 season Robinson scored in double figures in 81 of 82 games.*

Right: *David Robinson blocked more than 300 shots in each of his first three seasons with the San Antonio Spurs, and led the NBA with 305 in 1992.*

Page 88: *"Mr. Robinson's Neighborhood" has taken on a two-fold meaning in the NBA – it is his territory around the basket, and the focal point for his popular anti-drug commercials. Robinson contributes both on the court and off: he donated $180,000 to the San Antonio branch of the "I Have a Dream" Foundation for scholarships, and donates 50 tickets to each home game for "Mr. Robinson's Neighborhood," a section of San Antonio's HemisFair for students selected by their teachers for academic achievement.*

DENNIS RODMAN

Right: Dennis Rodman, nicknamed "The Worm," is a hard-edged player who cares more about playing defense than scoring points, and carved a unique niche for himself as an NBA All-Star. He uses his great quickness and unusual leaping ability to grab rebounds or block shots.

Below: At 6' 8", 210 pounds, Rodman does not have great size and bulk for a forward, but desire and athletic ability have made him a prodigious rebounder. He led the NBA for the first time in 1992, becoming the first player since 7' 1" Wilt Chamberlain to average more than 18 rebounds a game. He accumulated more than 4,000 rebounds in his first six seasons.

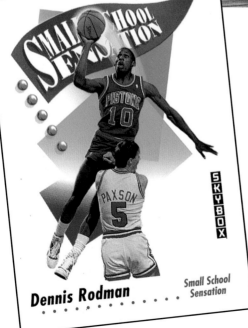

Position: Forward   **Birth Date:** May 13, 1961
College: SW Oklahoma State   **Height:** 6' 8"
Drafted: Detroit, 2nd Rd. ('86)   **Weight:** 210

He is nicknamed "The Worm," and he's been known to sculpt "Wild Thing" on the back of his scalp. Dennis Rodman is an unusual person, to say the least.

He also is a basketball phenomenon. His game is rebounding – pure and simple. In both 1991 and 1992, he exceeded 1,000 rebounds for the season. In 1992 he led the NBA in rebounding.

Not bad for someone who never even played high school basketball. But all he does is play hard every night and totally disrupt the opposition's game.

"Dennis not only is a very smart player," noted former Pistons coach Chuck Daly, "but he is very strong and a superbly conditioned athlete. There may be 150 guys in the NBA with the same fine athletic skills to do what he does, but they don't. What it really comes down to is desire and hard work."

RON SEIKALY

Position: Center
College: Syracuse
Drafted: Miami, 1st Rd. ('88)

Birth Date: May 10, 1965
Height: 6′ 11″
Weight: 252

Ron Seikaly, center for the Miami Heat, is one of the NBA's rebounding elite – a force so dominant under the basket that opponents construct game plans to try to circumvent him.

Seikaly is a native of Beirut, Lebanon, and went to high school in Athens, Greece. He came to Syracuse and helped the Orangemen to the NCAA championship game against Indiana in 1987, where they lost on a last-second shot. However, he became only the third college player ever to achieve 1,000 points and 1,000 rebounds, and was second in career blocked shots.

While he started out in the NBA with some good

Left: *Ron Seikaly has become one of the most improved players in the NBA since being chosen in the first round by the Miami Heat in 1988. He had to battle his way through his team's expansion growth, and each season leads his team in rebounds and blocked shots.*

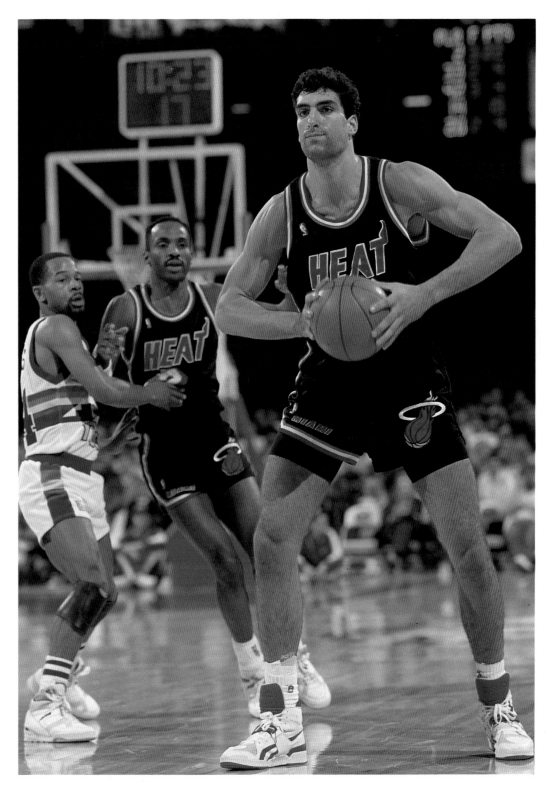

offensive and rebounding numbers, the focus of his game, with some help from former Boston all-pro center Dave Cowens, has shifted to rebounding. Consider:

• In his rookie 1989 season, he established a franchise record by averaging seven rebounds a game, highest among all of the NBA's draft picks that season. He started 62 of the 78 games he played and averaged 7½ rebounds in those games.

• In his second season, his rebound total improved from 549 to 766 and his average jumped to more than 10 per game, sixth highest in the NBA.

• In 1991, while turning in six 20+ rebound games en route to 709 in an injury-shortened season, he averaged 11 rebounds per game.

• By his fourth season, he pulled down 934, nearly 12 a game – again the sixth highest in the NBA. That not only broke his 1990 season mark, but also set team records for both offensive (307) and defensive (627) rebounds.

This does not mean Seikaly is a one-dimensional player. He has also improved his offense so that he is now one of the NBA's top centers. For example, in 1991 he turned in a pair of 30/20 games – 30 points and 20 rebounds – and they were the first in Miami's history.

The following season, against Detroit and Dennis Rodman, he was the first player in his team's history ever to play all 48 minutes and he scored 20 points with 18 rebounds and blocked six shots.

JOHN STOCKTON

Position: Guard
College: Gonzaga
Drafted: Utah, 1st Rd. ('84)

Birth Date: March 26, 1962
Height: 6′ 1″
Weight: 175

BARCELONA '92

JOHN STOCKTON

John Stockton plays basketball the old-fashioned way – he would rather give than receive.

Passing the ball is Stockton's principal skill, one that made him a unanimous pick for the 1992 Olympic team. Stockton has become the NBA's most prolific assist-maker, setting an NBA season record of 1,164 in 1991 (he broke his own record), and he is the only player ever to have as many as five consecutive seasons with 1,000 assists.

In so doing, he runs the offense of the Utah Jazz as a conductor directs his musicians. He demands offensive discipline in running his team's sets and he knows where everyone should be on the floor. He is very adept at setting up players for open shots, getting the ball to them at the right spot and at the right time.

His own offensive and defensive abilities often are

Right: *John Stockton was named to the 1992 U.S. Olympic team.*

Below: *Stockton drives past the Warriors' All-Star, Tim Hardaway.*

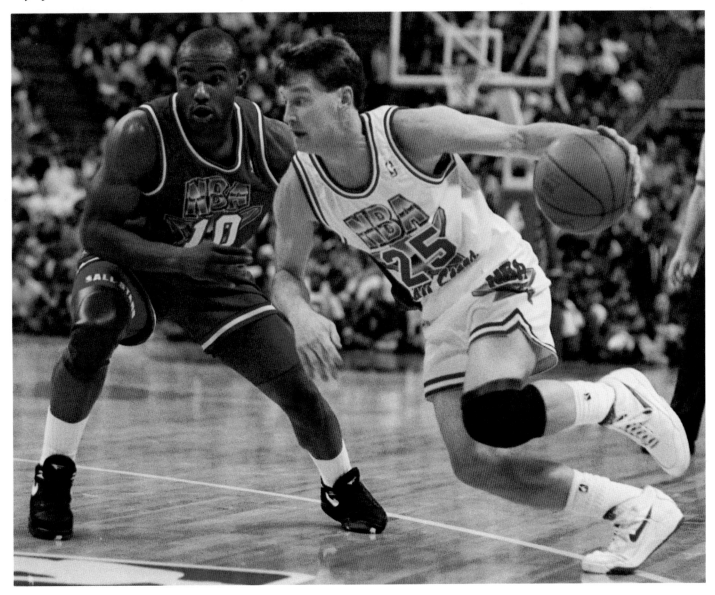

overlooked because when he first joined the Jazz, his reputation was forged on his play-making ability. But he is also a consistent double-figure scorer and one of the NBA's all-time leaders in steals. Play him too tightly and he will dump the ball to a shooter; back off, and he has enough quickness to dart through an opening and score. He has developed a neat trick of seeming to put himself out of position and then zipping back into the play to steal the ball.

What impresses teammates and foes alike is Stockton's total dedication to helping his team. "That's the kind of person he's been since he started to play for the Jazz," says his coach, Jerry Sloan. "That's why the other players like to play with him. He's a willing giver to this game and to his teammates, and you can't take those things lightly."

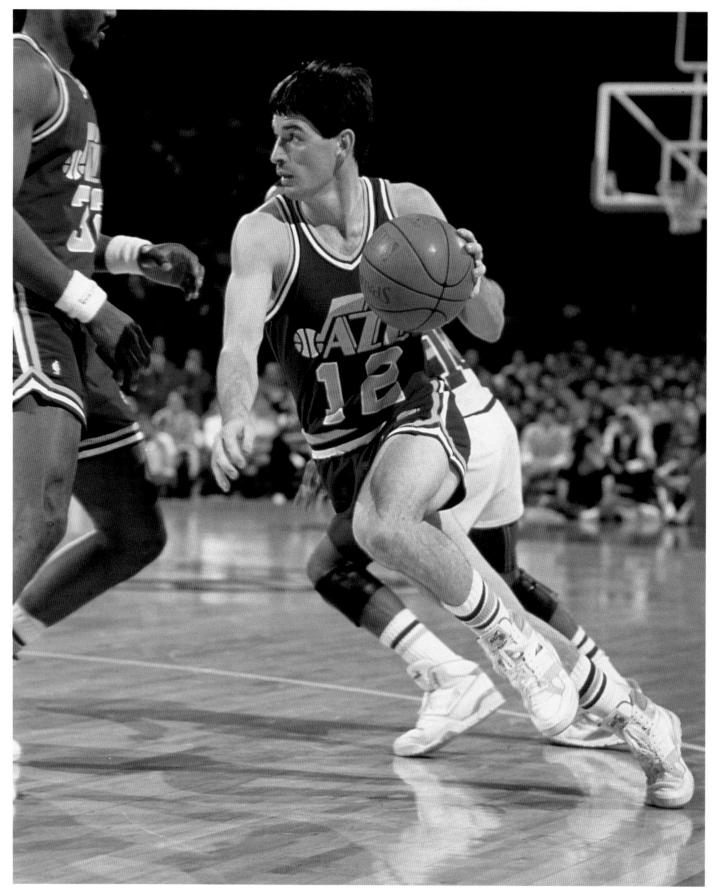

Opposite: *Many in the NBA believe that John Stockton and Karl Malone are the best guard-forward tandem in the NBA.*

Above: *Stockton is masterful in the way that he directs Utah's offense, particularly with his trigger-quick passing.*

Left: *Stockton had five consecutive seasons with 1,100 or more assists.*

Page 96: *Stockton's great passing and his ability to steal the ball have overshadowed his good offensive shooting, particularly his ability to move to the basket, or stop and pop a quick jump shot.*

ISIAH THOMAS

Position: Guard	**Birth Date:** April 30, 1961
College: Indiana	**Height:** 6' 1"
Drafted: Detroit, 1st Rd. ('81)	**Weight:** 185

"There isn't anything that Isiah Thomas can't do or doesn't do on a basketball court," Golden State Warriors coach Don Nelson once said. And no one has ever disagreed.

Isiah Lord Thomas III bypassed two seasons of eligibility for Bobby Knight at the University of Indiana in 1981, after helping the Hoosiers to the NCAA title that year, and at age 20, he became the first block of a rebuilding Detroit Pistons franchise that eventually won back-to-back NBA championships in 1989 and 1990.

In so doing, he became one of those few players who has reached such stature in the game that he is known simply by his first name. His soft, boyish features belie his fierce competitiveness.

There is nothing he would rather do than play the game. "I'm in love with basketball," he once said. "It's my release, my outlet. If I get mad, I go shoot. It's my freedom. It's my security, my high. When I'm playing,

Above: *Before joining the Pistons, Isiah Thomas was an All-America player under coach Bobby Knight at the University of Indiana in 1981. He helped the Hoosiers win the NCAA basketball championship that season, and was chosen the tournament's Most Valuable Player.*

Right: *Thomas relinquished his remaining college eligibility after the Hoosiers' NCAA championship season, and was the Pistons' second pick in the 1981 NBA draft. He displayed his great ballhandling skills immediately, and was selected for the all-rookie team in 1982.*

Left: *Isiah Thomas was an immediate star in the NBA, being selected to the league's All-NBA first team three consecutive seasons – 1984-85-86; and he made the all-second team in 1983, just his second season, and again in 1987.*

Below: *Thomas was named to the 1980 U.S. Olympic team but did not play because the U.S. boycotted the Games. In the NBA, he was selected to the Eastern Conference All-Star team for eight straight seasons. He was the game's Most Valuable Player in 1984 and 1986.*

Right: *Thomas is renowned for his great ballhandling skills. In each of his first 10 seasons, he led the Pistons in assists, accumulating more than 8,000 assists during that time, plus another 1,000 in post-season play. He led the NBA with 1,123 in 1985.*

Right: *Isiah Thomas faces Magic Johnson in the 1992 All-Star Game. Thomas helped to direct the Detroit Pistons to a pair of NBA championships in 1989 and 1990 with his all-around passing and shooting. He was selected as MVP of the 1990 playoff victory over Portland, and in 1988 he scored a record 25 points in one quarter against the Lakers.*

I'm nowhere. Nothing else exists. Nothing else matters. I just let it flow."

And that is how he plays the game. He is an on-the-move choreographer, using a myriad of graceful spins and jumps. His cat-like quickness gets him down the narrowest path along a baseline before a defender can respond.

He controls the Pistons' offense, dashing off passes with a flick of his wrists, and threading the ball into nearly impossible spaces – if he isn't zipping to the basket and laying the ball through the hoop himself with the gentlest of finger rolls.

Pat Riley, when coaching the Los Angeles Lakers, once painted this accurate profile of Isiah: "Can drive, penetrate, create . . . tough little kid. I love him because he's a spontaneous, creative player who makes things happen. . . . He is the prototype point guard who can play two ways. He can set people up or come at you. His nature is to attack."

Thomas is the only player in NBA history to start on the NBA All-Star team in each of his first five seasons, and twice, in 1984 and 1986, he was chosen MVP of that star-studded event. In the 1986 game he had 30 points, 10 assists and 5 steals, and Riley, coach of the losing West team, noted that Thomas had the perfect showcase for his considerable talents.

"Games like All-Star Games are freewheeling, footloose and fancy-free, and Isiah excels at that style," Riley said. "In a 94-foot game, where anything goes, he is probably the best because he can sustain a quick game for six or seven minutes."

And he can sustain a team for much, much longer.

OTIS THORPE

Position: Forward
College: Providence
Drafted: Kansas City, 1st Rd. ('84)

Birth Date: Aug. 5, 1962
Height: 6′ 10″
Weight: 236

By the time Otis Thorpe joined the Houston Rockets in a 1988 trade, he had already distinguished himself in NBA play. At Kansas City he had made the NBA's all-rookie team while scoring more than 20 points 13 times; in Sacramento, he was the 1987 team's Player of the Year, scoring in double figures in 61 straight games; and in his final season with the Kings he was one of just five NBA players who averaged double figures in both scoring and rebounding, finishing 16th in scoring and ninth in rebounds, while starting every game.

With the Rockets, he has become one of the pre-eminent NBA power forwards, made the All-Star team and is en route to establishing NBA records for playing in consecutive games.

"Otis is a blue-collar worker, who brings his hard hat and lunch bucket to a game," Don Chaney, his former Rockets coach, once said. "There is always room for someone like that in this game."

Below left: *Otis Thorpe is Houston's most accurate field goal shooter ever.*

Below right: *Thorpe averages about 17 points and 10 rebounds a game.*

DOUG WEST

Position: Guard   **Birth Date:** May 27, 1967
College: Villanova   **Height:** 6' 6"
Drafted: Minnesota, 2nd Rd. ('89)   **Weight:** 200

Doug West has been asked to do a lot during his NBA career.

His first coach with the Minnesota Timberwolves, Bill Musselman, called him the best athlete in the 1989 draft. Then he made him an out-of-position defensive specialist, though West had left Villanova as the third all-time scorer. When Jimmy Rodgers became head coach, West was called on to play the number two guard spot, then point guard, in 1992.

Obviously, West is a very adaptable player. Despite his collegiate offensive credentials, he dedicated himself to a defensive role under Musselman without any complaints. He was just as avid to accept Rodgers's "inside-outside" philosophy, feeding the big men in the low post while increasing his offensive contributions. West has shown that he is much more comfortable as a "contributor" than as a "go-to" guy.

"If I had to pick one guy off our team who is the most coachable, it is Doug West," said Minnesota assistant coach Sidney Lowe.

Left: *Doug West is a constant blur of motion during a game, as the Los Angeles Lakers discovered when they tried to stop him on a drive. He is a graceful athlete who was given a top defensive role early in his NBA career before being allowed more offensive responsibilities.*

DOMINIQUE WILKINS

Right: *Dominique Wilkins displays his style in slam-dunk competition. Wilkins is the Hawks' all-time leading scorer, and led the team in scoring in nine of his first ten seasons. He also led the NBA in 1986 with a 30.3 points per game mark, and was second in both 1987 and 1988. He averaged less than 20 points only once – in his rookie season – and he has been his team's top scorer in over 500 games.*

Below: *Wilkins's given name is Jacques Dominique Wilkins; he was born in France when his father was serving with the U.S. Air Force. He was an All-America player at the University of Georgia, then a unanimous choice for the NBA's 1983 all-rookie team. His brother Gerald has played for the New York Knicks.*

Position: Forward **Birth Date:** Jan. 12, 1960
College: Georgia **Height:** 6′ 8″
Drafted: New Orleans, 1st Rd. ('82) **Weight:** 200

Dominique Wilkins must believe in living on the brink.

After a great high school career at Washington, North Carolina, he bypassed the considerable pleas from that state's great basketball schools – and decided instead to enroll at the University of Georgia. That decision so incensed the state's basketball fanatics that he and his family received threats.

He became Georgia's greatest player and was known as the "Human Highlights Film" before deciding to leave early. He was drafted by the New Orleans Jazz, who were then in the process of moving to Salt Lake City, and traded him to the Atlanta Hawks.

Still, Wilkins's career remained unfulfilled, often seeming short of his potential. In 1987 the Hawks picked up center Moses Malone and high-scoring guard Reggie Theus, and Wilkins was at the top of his game for the next couple of seasons – starting in All-Star Games and coming in second in NBA scoring for two consecutive years.

But when asked why there couldn't be more, former Atlanta coach Mike Fratello said: "What you see is what you get," meaning that Wilkins's worth was not measured by defense, rebounding, or shot selection.

Wilkins got the message. His shot selection improved, he moved the ball around to other players, and became more intense on defense.

"If people learned to respect the way I played, they must understand that maturity had much to do with it," he said. "I really didn't change much of my overall game, I just paid more attention to all of the individual parts."

Atlanta coach Bob Weiss says that Wilkins has achieved everything asked of him. "I thought he was an athletic scorer who could up the numbers but I wasn't sure how much he could help other people," Weiss

Above: *Wilkins was a first team selection for the All-NBA team in 1986, and made the second team in 1989. A natural shooter, he has worked to improve his passing and rebounding skills.*

Left: *Dominique started for the Eastern Conference in the All-Star Game in 1987-88-89, and had a string of six consecutive appearances broken when he was injured midway through the 1992 season.*

Opposite: *Wilkins has battled the Chicago Bulls' Michael Jordan for several scoring titles. Michael once complained to him during a game that he was trying to take the title from him. "No I'm not," Wilkins replied. "It's your NBA title that I want."*

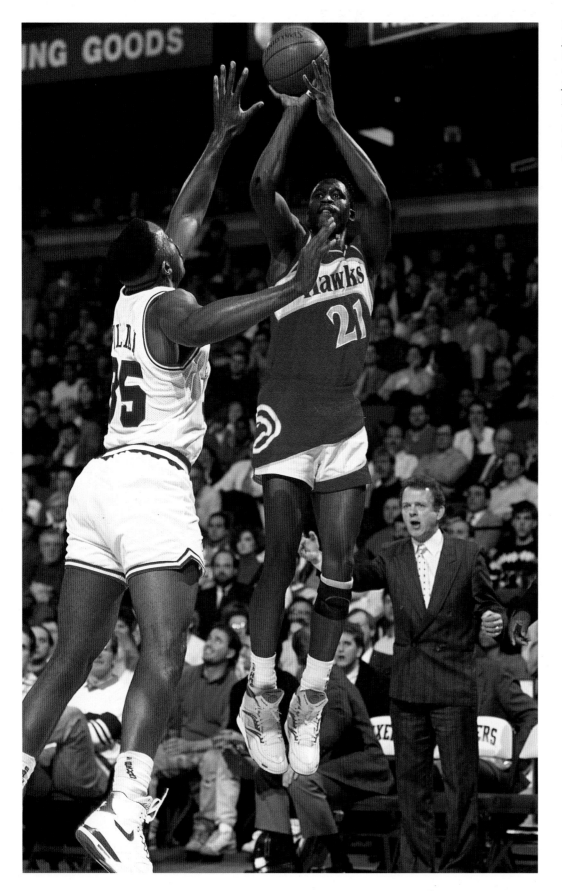

Left: *Wilkins is renowned for his ability to get the ball into tight places around the basket, and he also has a fine shooting touch for pull-up jumpers. Dominique has averaged more than 26 points and seven rebounds a game during his career.*

said. "But I think he wanted to get rid of that reputation and be recognized as a complete player, and not just a super talent. And he's done that in a lot of ways, like breaking his habit of leaking out to get on the fast break. He stayed to battle on the boards and that gave him more rebounds."

How many more? Wilkins grabbed a team-high 732 in 1991, including 471 on defense, to lead the Hawks for the first time in those categories while continuing his scoring leadership.

He went back to the brink in 1992, when on the night he was expected to become only the 17th NBA player ever to score 20,000 points, he tore his achilles tendon and missed the rest of the season. Only three players ever achieved the 20,000-point mark faster – Wilt Chamberlain, Kareem Abdul-Jabbar and Oscar Robertson – but Weiss says that there is no telling just how high he will soar during the rest of his NBA career.

KEVIN WILLIS

Position: Forward   **Birth Date:** Sept. 6, 1962
College: Michigan State   **Height:** 7' 0"
Drafted: Atlanta, 1st Rd. ('84)   **Weight:** 235

For most of the first seven years of his pro career with the Atlanta Hawks, Kevin Willis was considered one of the NBA's greatest underachievers. Not any more. With All-Star recognition now on his resume, he has gotten new respect from opponents and teammates alike.

For most of those first seven seasons, he was lackadaisical about contesting rebounds. That's all changed now. He has gone on rebounding binges, including one 17-game stretch during the 1992 season in which he collected more than 20 in eight of those games.

"I knew I could rebound," he says now. "My new figures are no fluke."

Above: *Kevin Willis was an All-Big Ten player at Michigan State before becoming the 11th player picked in the first round of the 1984 draft. During his career with the Hawks, he has averaged over 13 points and nearly 10 rebounds per game.*

Right: *Willis is a force on the backboards when he gets after that part of his game. Here he skies over Gerald Henderson, then with Milwaukee. Clifford Ray, a fine rebounding center during the seventies, summed up Willis's play: "He plays like he's from the old school. He has the mentality to rebound – 'everything is mine.'"*

Those around the Hawks find Willis's turnaround a bit unbelievable. For years, he tortured then-coach Mike Fratello with his inconsistent play. He did the same to Weiss until his new coach benched him for long stretches during the 1991 season, and after the season matters reached such a low point that the Hawks tried to trade him. Even early in the 1992 season, Weiss sat him down during a game against the Phoenix Suns.

At that point, Willis woke up. He took to heart Weiss's admonition that he had to pick up the rebounding load once carried by Moses Malone, and that the only way he would get more playing time – and minutes in a game are an NBA player's most valuable currency – was to produce Malone-type numbers.

He did all his coach asked him, and when teammate Dominique Wilkins suffered an achilles injury that prevented him from playing in the 1992 All-Star Game, Willis was picked to replace him.

"It's timing and a lot of other things," Willis says. "I learned a lot from watching Moses Malone . . . and I just try to apply my own quickness and physical strength."

But he also has added much of the tenacity that made Malone one of the NBA's great players – and taken together, the Hawks believe they now have the "real" Kevin Willis.

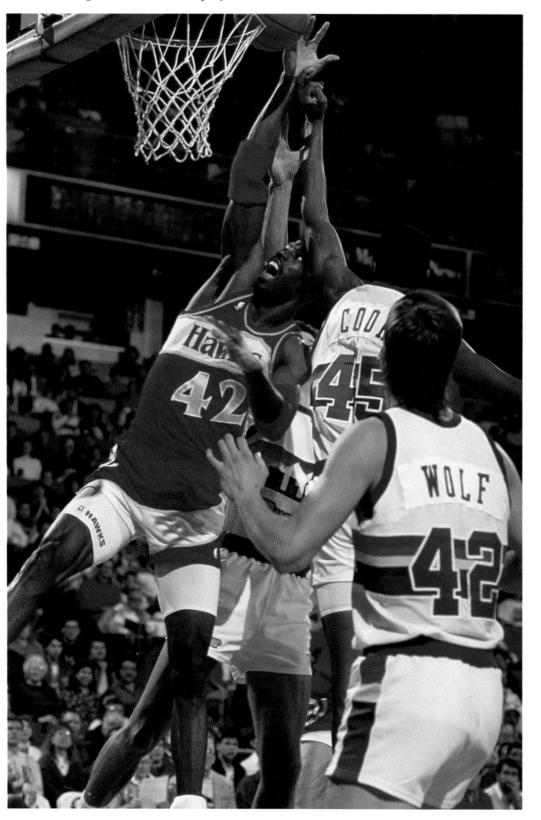

Left: *Willis overpowers Joe Wolf and Tony Cook of Denver. The big forward has led the Hawks in rebounding in more than 200 games. During the 1986 season, he twice had 21-rebound games, and he has pulled down more than 5,000 during his NBA career. His coach, Bobby Weiss, compares him to two of the NBA's greatest rebounders ever – Bill Russell and Wilt Chamberlain, against whom Weiss played during his career.*

Opposite: *Willis realized his full potential during the 1992 season when he averaged more than 18 points and 15 rebounds to take up the slack after Dominique Wilkins was injured at mid-season. Willis also replaced him in the All-Star Game.*

JAMES WORTHY

Position: Forward	**Birth Date:** Feb. 27, 1961
College: North Carolina	**Height:** 6' 9"
Drafted: L.A. Lakers, 1st Rd. ('82)	**Weight:** 225

"He's always been number one," said former Phoenix coach Cotton Fitzsimmons when discussing James Worthy. "He has been an underrated player as far as the Lakers are concerned because they had Kareem Abdul-Jabbar and Magic Johnson. But he's always been a sensational forward."

Worthy has been on three NBA championship teams in L.A., the last for which he delivered a sensational seventh-game performance against Detroit in 1989, when he had 36 points, 16 rebounds and 10 assists.

He stepped up to fill the team's leadership role after Magic Johnson retired in 1992. "In certain situations when we need a shot, I feel I can either get it, or find the open man with a pass," he said. "It's what I learned from Kareem and Magic."

Above: *James Worthy played on three of the Lakers' championship teams in the eighties, and was MVP of the 1988 NBA playoffs. As an All-America at North Carolina, he had helped the Tar Heels to the 1982 NCAA championship and was named MVP of that tournament, too.*

Right: *Worthy's trademark is his smooth drive to the basket.*

Opposite: *Worthy was the first player picked in the 1982 draft – he and Magic Johnson are the only two Lakers since 1960 to share that distinction – and he was the team's No. 2 scorer for five consecutive seasons before leading the team in 1991-92. Worthy has averaged more than 18 points a game since coming to the Lakers.*

INDEX